METUSELA ALBERT

THE
BIBLE
CONTRADICTS

BUT WHAT GOD SAID TO THE PROPHET(S)
DID NOT CONTRADICT

To order additional copies of this book, contact:
Xlibris
844-714-8691
www.Xlibris.com
Orders@Xlibris.com

ISBN: 979-8-3694-1176-6 (sc)
ISBN: 979-8-3694-1175-9 (e)

Print information available on the last page

Rev. date: 11/21/2023

CONTENTS

PART A – THE TRUTH ABOUT "JESUS" IN THE OLD TESTAMENT.

INTRODUCTION..v

CHAPTER 1. JESUS WAS THE ELOHIM (YAHWEH / JEHOVAH) WHO CREATED
            HEAVEN AND EARTH...1

CHAPTER 2. JESUS WAS THE ELOHIM (YAHWEH / JEHOVAH) OF ABRAHAM. 4

CHAPTER 3. JESUS WAS THE ELOHIM (YAHWEH / JEHOVAH) WHO WROTE THE
            TEN COMMANDMENTS. 8

CHAPTER 4. ELOHIM (YAHWEH /JEHOVAH) INCARNATED INTO HUMAN FLESH
            AND WAS CALLED – JESUS, THE SON OF GOD...11

CHAPTER 5. ELOHIM (YAHWEH / JEHOVAH) DID NOT HAVE A SON IN HEAVEN
            CALLED – JESUS. 13

•••

PART B – THE CONTRADICTIONS IN THE NEW TESTAMENT.

CHAPTER 6. JOHN'S CONTRADICTION IN JOHN 1:1-14 AND JOHN 3:16. 24

CHAPTER 7. JOHN'S CONTRADICTION IN 1 JOHN 4:1-19 AND 1 JOHN 5:7....................34

CHAPTER 8. PAUL'S CONTRADICTION IN ROMANS 8:34. 36

CHAPTER 9. PAUL'S CONTRADICTION IN 1 CORINTHIANS 8:6. 37

CHAPTER 10. PAUL'S CONTRADICTION IN COLOSSIANS 1:15 -18. 39

CHAPTER 11. PAUL'S CONTRADICTION IN 1 TIMOTHY 2:5. 41

CHAPTER 12. PAUL'S CONTRADICTION IN HEBREWS 1:1-2 43

CHAPTER 13. PETER'S CONTRADICTION IN 1 PETER 1:3..45

CHAPTER 14. JOHN'S CONTRADICTION IN REVELATION 1:8-11. 46

CHAPTER 15.   THE CONTRADICTION BY JAMES. 50

CHAPTER 16.   WHO RESURRECTED JESUS? NOTE PAUL'S CONTRADICTION. 51

CHAPTER 17.   WHO IS THE HOLY SPIRIT? 53

CONCLUSION 55

INTRODUCTION

I often say, "When you know <u>THE TRUTH</u>, you will easily know the ERROR(S). But if you don't know THE TRUTH, you will <u>not</u> know the ERROR(S)."

First, you must know "THE TRUTH", in order to know the CONTRADICTION of the BIBLE.

....

In order to understand <u>HOW</u> the BIBLE contradicts, first - you must understand "THE TRUTH" about GOD. Here are five questions to help analyze the TRUTH about GOD.

1. Who created heaven and earth? Was it the Son of GOD or GOD? Read Genesis 1:1.

2. Who was the GOD of Abraham who created heaven and earth? Read Genesis 12:1-3; John 8:56-58.

3. Did the GOD of Abraham have a Son in heaven called - JESUS? If yes, then <u>when</u> did the Son of GOD exist? And <u>how</u> did the Son of GOD exist?

4. How many Divine BEINGS existed in heaven before the angels were created? One or Two or Three?

5. Was JESUS self-existent? Or Was JESUS born by the FATHER before the angels existed?

6. If JESUS was born by the FATHER, then He could not have been ALPHA and Omega. True OR False?

Those questions above must be answered well, in order to avoid all Confusion and Contradictions.

....

NOTE: The <u>first five Chapters</u> of <u>this Book</u> were designed to clarify "THE TRUTH" about GOD, so that when you read the New Testament, you should be able to notice the contradictions made by the writers like John, Peter, James, Paul, etc. without any difficult.

....

I did not say, "GOD contradicts."

I said, "The Bible contradicts."

You need to understand the difference so that you <u>are not</u> confused.

....

Please pray to have an open mind before you read <u>this Book</u>. It will surely change your mind to understand <u>THE TRUTH</u> about JESUS, that perhaps, you may have <u>not</u> been told before.

....

SO, WHAT IS <u>THE TRUTH ABOUT JESUS?</u>

<u>THE TRUTH IS</u>: JESUS was the Almighty GOD (ELOHIM / YAHWEH / JEHOVAH) who <u>created</u> heaven and earth in six days and rested on the seventh day (the Sabbath).

(Genesis 1:1-31; 2:1-3; Exodus 3:13-14; 6:1-3; 20:1-17; Isaiah 43:10-11; 44:6,24; 49:16; John 5:39,46; 8:56-58; Revelation 21:6-7).

....

After having said that, we will TEST the NEW TESTAMENT writers by that truth.

NOTE: JESUS WAS THE **ONLY GOD** THAT EXISTED IN HEAVEN BEFORE HE CREATED THE ANGELS.

In heaven, JESUS was <u>*not*</u> the Son of GOD when HE created the angels. Before JESUS created the angels in heaven, <u>HE alone</u> existed as GOD.

In other words, there was <u>no such thing</u> as GOD had a begotten Son called JESUS in heaven before the angels were created. And there was <u>no</u> third person called – HOLY SPIRIT that existed before the angels were created.

THIS POINT MUST BE UNDERSTOOD CLEARLY FROM THE BEGINNING.

In heaven, there was **no** such thing as a Trinity GOD or a Triune GOD that existed before the angels existed.

....

GOD alone existed in heaven before HE created the angels.

There was <u>no</u> such thing as <u>two divine persons</u> nor <u>three divine persons</u> existed in heaven *before* the angels were created.

I repeat again, there was <u>no such thing</u> as GOD had a begotten Son called JESUS in heaven *before* the angels were created.

I reiterate the Point – "GOD was the <u>only divine BEING</u> that existed in heaven from eternity *before* He created the angels. That GOD was JESUS, even though He was not called – JESUS, back then. The name JESUS was only being mentioned in the New Testament."

....

Furthermore, when Lucifer and one-third of the angels sinned against GOD in heaven, HE threw them out of heaven to this planet earth. They were **not** allowed to stay in heaven nor to return. They sinned against GOD, **not** against <u>the</u> Son of GOD because there was NO Son of GOD in heaven.

NOTE: GOD did <u>not</u> cast Lucifer and the fallen angels to any other planet, except to this earth. They had <u>no</u> access to the other planets. They were restricted to our planet earth because the PLAN OF SALVATION for mankind will take place at CALVARY in our planet. . . . It was in our planet earth that JESUS would come in human flesh and die at CALVARY, as our Sin Bearer / Savior. And JESUS fulfilled the plan accordingly.

The PLAN OF SALVATION for man was made before GOD casted Lucifer and the fallen angels to our earth.

....

NOTE: IN HEAVEN, GOD WAS <u>NOT</u> NAMED JESUS. AND IN THE OLD TESTAMENT TIME, GOD WAS NOT NAMED JESUS, EITHER. NOT UNTIL THE INCARNATION AT BETHLEHEM THROUGH MARY, THAT THE NAME "JESUS" WAS MENTIONED – (Luke 1:35). Virgin Mary was told to name the baby – JESUS.

....

While Lucifer and the <u>fallen angels</u> were present in our empty planet earth, JESUS created the things in our planet. HE started by creating <u>the light</u> (Genesis 1:1-3), then the sky, the sun, the moon, the stars, the water, the animals, birds, fishes, insects, the trees, the tree of Life, the tree of the Knowledge of Good and Evil, and Adam and Eve.

Of course, JESUS created the weekly cycle of seven days. Till today, the weekly cycle around the world, is still seven days. The Sabbath was the seventh day of the week, given to Adam and Eve. It was going to be part of the written Ten Commandments to be given through Moses at Mount Sinai.

IMPORTANT POINT: The Plan of Salvation was already made *before* JESUS created the things in our planet earth, and Adam and Eve. It is our planet earth that JESUS would come and be born through Mary at Bethlehem, and die at Calvary, as our Sin Bearer / Savior. This reveals GOD'S omniscience (foreknowledge) and love.

DON'T MISS THIS: JESUS WAS NOT THE SON OF GOD WHEN HE CREATED THE ANGELS IN HEAVEN. HE WAS NOT THE SON OF GOD WHEN HE CREATED ALL THINGS IN OUR PLANET EARTH IN SIX DAYS, AND RESTED ON THE SEVENTH DAY (THE SABBATH).

UNDERSTAND THIS: JESUS ONLY BECAME THE SON OF GOD BY THE INCARNATION PROCESS THROUGH MARY AT BETHLEHEM, TO SAVE THE WORLD FROM SIN AND ETERNAL DEATH. THERE WAS ONLY ONE PERSON IN HEAVEN, NOT EVEN TWO OR THREE PERSONS.

NOTE: THE HOLY SPIRIT WAS NOT A PERSON NOR A THIRD PERSON.

GET THIS: JESUS WAS THE PERSON, AND THE HOLY SPIRIT WAS THE SPIRIT OF JESUS.

KEEP THIS IN MIND: JESUS was not a TRINITY GOD, nor a TRIUNE GOD. HE had no beginning and no ending. HE was the ALPHA and OMEGA. HE existed by Himself from eternity. HE was NOT begat by anyone. HE was GOD the FATHER, the GOD of Abraham, who incarnated into human flesh through Mary at Bethlehem, and became the Son of GOD. HE was not GOD the Son. There was no such thing as GOD the SON, OR GOD the HOLY SPIRIT.

POINT: There was NO such thing as GOD the FATHER gave birth to a Son called JESUS in heaven from eternity before the angels existed. In other words, GOD the Father did not have a begotten Son called JESUS in heaven, before the angels existed.

The notion that GOD the FATHER had a begotten Son in heaven before the angels existed came in the New Testament by the New Testament writers because they did not know that JESUS was the GOD of Abraham in the Old Testament.

WHAT IS THE TRUTH???

- **THE TRUTH IS:**
- **JESUS was the CREATOR, (ELOHIM / YAHWEH / JEHOVAH) who became the Almighty GOD of Abraham, called – "I AM THAT I AM".**
- **HE alone created heaven and earth in six days and rested on the seventh day.**
- **HE later incarnated into human flesh through Mary at Bethlehem, in order for Him to die at Calvary, as our Sin Bearer/ Savior.**
- (Genesis 1:1-31; 2:1-3; Exodus 3:13-14; 6:1-3; 20:1-3; 8-11; Isaiah 43:10-11; 44:6, 24; 49:16; John 5:39,46; 8:56-58; Revelation 21:6-7).
- **JESUS WAS NOT, AND IS NOT, A TRINITY GOD.**

Compiled by: Metusela F. Albert.

REMEMBER THIS: Once you come to a good understanding that JESUS was the only GOD (ELOHIM / YAHWEH / JEHOVAH) of the Old Testament Prophets, only then you can understand the CONTRADICTION of the BIBLE by the New Testament writers.

....

What the New Testament writers *wrote* about GOD the FATHER, JESUS (the Son), and the HOLY SPIRIT, must be tested by what GOD said about Himself, to the Prophets in the Old Testament.

....

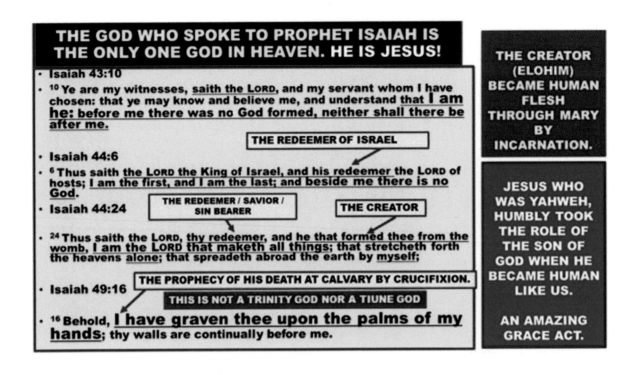

IMPORTANT INFORMATION ABOUT THE BIBLE.

The BIBLE is <u>a Book</u> that is made up of 66 Books; 39 in the Old Testament and 27 in the New Testament. It <u>contains</u> NOT only the actual words spoken by GOD (ELOHIM / YAHWEH / JEHOVAH), but also <u>the actual words spoken by OTHERS</u>.

For example, the actual words spoken by <u>others besides GOD,</u> refer to the words of Lucifer (Satan), the words of the angel Gabriel, the words of the Prophet(s), and the words of ordinary men and women who were <u>not</u> Prophets.

Here are some names of men and women who had their words recorded in the Old Testament – Amram, Jochebed, Aaron, Miriam, Jethro, King Pharoah, Queen Esther, Naaman, Mordecai, Rahab (the Prostitute), Joab, King Nebuchadnezzar, King Saul, King David, King Solomon, Jeroboam, Rehoboam, Jesse, King Ahab, Queen Jezebel, King Jehosaphat, etc. Even though their words were recorded in the Bible, however, their words were <u>not</u> GOD'S word.

In the New Testament, the words of these people - Pilate, Judas, Lazarus, Mary, Peter, James, John, Paul, Barnabas, Timothy, Jude, The Thief on the Cross, The Roman Soldier, etc., were also recorded in the BIBLE. . . . But their words were <u>*not*</u> the spoken words of GOD, unless they were making a <u>direct quote</u> about what GOD said. That is a different issue.

PLEASE UNDERSTAND THIS: Paul wrote 14 letters to the Churches *about* GOD (the FATHER), JESUS (the SON), and the HOLY SPIRIT. . . . Paul's words were *not* the spoken word of GOD.

....

The only time that Paul had an encounter with GOD was when JESUS, the GOD of Abraham, spoke to him on the road to Damacus while he was on his way to destroy the *believers* in JESUS CHRIST – (Acts 9).

DON'T FORGET THIS. Paul's words were *not* the word of GOD. But JESUS' words were GOD'S word.

Remember, JESUS who came in human flesh through Mary at Bethlehem, was the GOD (ELOHIM / YAHWEH / JEHOVAH) of Abraham who spoke to Moses at the burning bush – Exodus 3:13-14; John 8:56-58.

//

TAKE NOTE OF THIS IMPORTANT POINT.

In the New Testament, when John, Peter, James, Paul and the others wrote *about* GOD, they were referring to the GOD of Abraham. Here is the thing. They did not know that JESUS who was born of Mary at Bethlehem was the GOD of Abraham in the Old Testament era. They did not understand the INCARNATION process that was prophesied in the Book of Isaiah – (Isaiah 7:14; 9:6). They believed that JESUS was a distinct being from the GOD of Abraham. They failed to understand that only one divine being existed in heaven. They believed that GOD the Father had a begotten Son called JESUS in heaven before the angels existed.

THE TRUTH IS - THERE WAS NO SUCH THING AS TWO DIVINE BEINGS NOR THREE, EXISTING IN HEAVEN. . . . ONLY ONE THAT EXISTS IN HEAVEN.

....

FURTHER EXPLANATION AND EXAMPLE:

When JESUS spoke to the Roman Governor called Pilate, JESUS' words were GOD'S word because HE was GOD, THE ALPHA AND OMEGA – Revelation 21:6-7.

....

JESUS WAS THE ONLY GOD. . . . HE was the Almighty GOD of Abraham. HE was the everlasting FATHER of the Children of Israel in the Old Testament.

Therefore, the words of JESUS in the New Testament were the words of GOD. But the words of Pilate, Judas, Lazarus, Mary, Peter, James, John, Paul and the others, as recorded in the BIBLE, were <u>not</u> the word of GOD.

THAT IS WHY IT IS <u>NOT</u> APPROPRIATE TO SAY – "THE BIBLE IS GOD'S WORD."

You <u>cannot</u> judge this BOOK by its COVER. I believe, the <u>TITLE</u> of this Book must be shocking to many of you *before* you read it. Remember, what GOD said did <u>not</u> contradict. It is the BIBLE that contradicts.

....

WHAT IS THE POINT?

When you read the Old Testament, try and find out the <u>actual words</u> that proceeded out of GOD'S mouth to the Prophet OR to whosoever. (Deuteronomy 8:1-3). Establish that as your main point about GOD'S word.

....

In the New Testament, the words of Zachariah and Elizabeth, the words of John the Baptist, the words of Judas, the words of Pilate, the words of Matthew, Mark, Luke, John, Peter, James, and Paul, were <u>not</u> the word of GOD. UNLESS they "quote" the exact words spoken by GOD to the Prophet OR the exact words of JESUS, said to whosoever.

....

THINK ABOUT THIS.

<u>Not</u> everything written in the Bible are GOD'S Word because the words of OTHERS were also recorded in the BIBLE. Therefore, the BIBLE is <u>not</u> GOD'S word. The BIBLE contains GOD'S words, and the words of Others.

It is <u>not</u> appropriate anymore nor Biblical to say "The BIBLE is GOD'S word." Our long time <u>Tradition</u> of saying, "THE BIBLE IS GOD'S WORD," has to change, especially after being enlightened. . . . . We cannot afford to continue making SATAN'S words written in the BIBLE to become GOD'S WORD.

TRADITION THAT IS WRONG, NEEDS TO CHANGE.

HOW TO SAY THE RIGHT THING ABOUT THE BIBLE?

We should say –

1. THE BIBLE <u>CONTAINS</u> THE WORDS OF GOD, AND THE WORDS OF OTHERS ALSO.

2. IN THE BIBLE, WE CAN READ GOD'S SPOKEN WORDS, AND THE WORDS OF OTHERS ALSO.

Dear folks, when you read the Bible, try and differentiate <u>what GOD said</u> from what the Prophets' and others said.

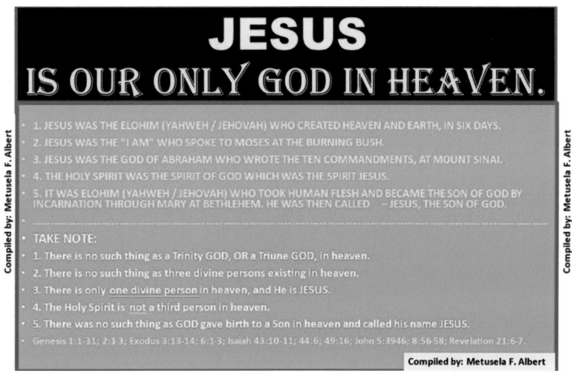

WHAT IS THE TRUTH?

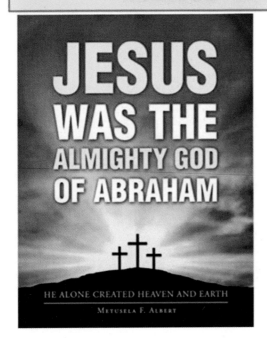

• Most Professed Christians and Protestant Churches have not understood yet that JESUS who became our Sin Bearer at Calvary (31 A.D.) was the Almighty God of Abraham who created heaven and earth.

CHAPTER 1

JESUS WAS THE ELOHIM (YAHWEH / JEHOVAH) WHO CREATED HEAVEN AND EARTH.

....

Scripture: Genesis 1:1-3 (KJV).

1 In the beginning **God** created the heaven and the earth.

² And the earth was without form and void, and darkness was upon the face of the deep. And the <u>Spirit of</u> God moved upon the face of the waters.

³ And **God** <u>said</u>, "<u>Let there be light</u>"; and there was light.

///

AN IMPORTANT QUESTION NEEDS TO BE ASKED.

QUESTION: WHO WAS THAT GOD WHO CREATED THE LIGHT IN GENESIS 1:1-3?

Let's read some Scriptures to help us answer the question.

1. In the New Testament, JESUS said in John 8:32, <u>I AM the light</u> of the world.

2. In John 5:46, JESUS said, "Had you believed <u>Moses</u>, you would have believed <u>Me</u>; <u>for Moses wrote about Me</u>."

3. And in John 8:58, JESUS said, "<u>Before Abraham was I AM</u>."

//

EXPLANATION

After reading those three Scriptures given above, we can conclude that JESUS was the ELOHIM / YAHWEH / JEHOVAH who created the light in Genesis 1:3.

John 8:12 gives us the answer. JESUS said, "I am the light of the world."

And Moses who wrote the Book of Genesis wrote about Him. He existed before Moses and Abraham. JESUS was the GOD of Abraham called – "I AM THAT I AM" who spoke to Moses at the burning bush – (Exodus 3:13-14; 6:1-3). HE wrote the Ten Commandments on two tablets of stone at Mount Sinai. JESUS was the GOD who spoke to the Prophets in the Old Testament.

....

Even though the Creator was not called JESUS in the Book of Genesis, however, Scripture explains itself. When JESUS created the light and everything, as recorded in Genesis 1:1-31; 2:1-3, He was not the Son of GOD because there was no such thing as GOD had a Son, then.

Genesis 1:1 did not say, "In the beginning, the Son of God created heaven and earth."

....

THE TRUTH versus THE ERROR.

THE TRUTH -
- Scripture: Genesis 1:1 (KJV) says.
- "In the beginning **God** created the heaven and the earth."
- ....
- NOTE: Genesis 1:1 - Does **NOT** say, "In the beginning the Son of God created the heaven and the earth."

THE ERROR
- Since Genesis 1:1 (KJV) - Does NOT SAY.
- "In the beginning <u>the Son of God</u> created the heaven and the earth, therefore, John 1:1 -3 and Colossians 1:13 -18 contradicted Genesis 1:1.

Compiled by: Metusela F. Albert

Remember, when you know the truth, you will know the error(S). Of course, John 1:1-3 contradicted Genesis 1:1-3.

HOW?

There was **no** Son of GOD mentioned in Genesis 1:1-3. At the time of Creation in the Book of Genesis Chapter 1, GOD did **not** have a Son in heaven called JESUS.

JESUS alone was the CREATOR. HE was **not** the Son of GOD when HE created heaven and earth.

Beware when you read John and Paul's writings about JESUS as the Son of GOD who created heaven and earth.

///

....

APPLICATION. Though GOD (ELOHIM / YAHWEH / JEHOVAH) was not called JESUS in the Old Testament, yet JESUS was <u>the same person</u> in the Old Testament era. HE was GOD the Father of the children of Israel in the Old Testament who later **incarnated** into human flesh through Mary at Bethlehem and was called – "JESUS". He was also called – "The Son of GOD" - (Luke 1:35).

....

JESUS WAS THE GOD WHO CREATED THE LIGHT.

- Genesis 1:1-3 (King James Version)
- 1 In the beginning <u>God created</u> the heaven and the earth.
- ² And the earth was without form and void, and darkness was upon the face of the deep. And the Spirit of God moved upon the face of the waters.
- ³ And <u>God said, "Let there be light</u>"; and there was light.

- John 8:12 – Jesus said,
- <u>I am</u> the light of the world.

- Further Reading – John 5:39, 46; 8:56-58.

COMPILED BY: METUSELA F. ALBERT .

CHAPTER 2

JESUS WAS THE ELOHIM (YAHWEH / JEHOVAH) OF ABRAHAM.

....

Genesis 12:1-3. (KJV).

- 1. Now <u>the Lord</u> had said unto Abram, "Get thee out of thy country, and from thy kindred and from thy father's house, unto a land <u>that I will show thee.</u>
- ² <u>And I will make of thee a great nation,</u> and <u>I will bless thee</u> and make thy name great; and thou shalt be a blessing.
- ³ <u>And I will bless them</u> that bless thee, and curse him that curseth thee; and in thee shall all families of the earth be blessed."

TAKE NOTE OF <u>THE SINGULAR PRONOUN</u> USED – "I", NOT "WE."

ABRAHAM'S GOD WAS <u>NOT</u> A TRINITY GOD.

- Genesis 12:1-3.
- 1. Now the LORD had said unto Abram, "Get thee out of thy country, and from thy kindred and from thy father's house, unto a land <u>that I will show thee.</u>
- ² <u>And I will make of thee a great nation,</u> and <u>I will bless thee</u> and make thy name great; and thou shalt be a blessing.
- ³ <u>And I will bless them</u> that bless thee, and curse him that curseth thee; and in thee shall all families of the earth be blessed."

DID YOU NOTICE THE SINGULAR PRONOUN USED FOR THE LORD GOD OF ABRAHAM WAS AN "I" ?????

THE "I" WAS MENTIONED 4 TIMES.

THIS WAS <u>NOT</u> A TRINITY GOD.

HE WAS JESUS – Read John 5:39, 46; 8:56-58.

Compiled by: Metusela F. Albert

4

EXPLANATION

It is important that we understand who the GOD of Abraham was. He was <u>not</u> a TRINITY GOD.

How would we know that the God of Abraham was <u>NOT</u> a Trinity GOD? Because of the singular <u>pronoun</u> used. The <u>pronoun</u> "I" was mentioned four (4) times, in three verses.

HOW WOULD WE KNOW THAT THE GOD OF ABRAHAM WAS JESUS?

1. Read Exodus 3:13-14 and Exodus 6:1-3.

2. Then Read John 5:39 and John 5:46.

3. Then read John 8:56-58.

NOTE: Those Scriptures pointed to only <u>one person</u> named - JESUS.

Allow Scripture to interpret itself. (Precept Upon Precept).

....

JESUS WAS THE GOD OF ABRAHAM – "THE I AM THAT I AM."

- Exodus 3:13-14

- [13] And Moses said unto God, "Behold, when I come unto the children of Israel and shall say unto them, 'The God of your fathers hath sent me unto you,' and they shall say to me, <u>'What is His name?'</u> what shall I say unto them?"

- [14] And God said unto Moses, <u>"I AM THAT I AM."</u> And He said, "Thus shalt thou say unto the children of Israel, <u>'I AM</u> hath sent me unto you.'"

- John 5:39 – JESUS said,

- "Search the Scriptures, for in them ye think ye have eternal life; and <u>it is they which testify of Me</u>.

JESUS WAS THE GOD OF ABRAHAM— "I AM THAT I AM."

- Exodus 3:13-14

- ¹³ And Moses said unto God, "Behold, when I come unto the children of Israel and shall say unto them, 'The God of your fathers hath sent me unto you,' and they shall say to me, 'What is His name?' what shall I say unto them?"

- ¹⁴ And God said unto Moses, "I AM THAT I AM." And He said, "Thus shalt thou say unto the children of Israel, 'I AM hath sent me unto you.'"

- John 5:46 – JESUS said,

- ⁴⁶ For had ye believed Moses, ye would have believed Me, for he wrote of Me.

THE GOD OF ABRAHAM (ELOHIM / YAHWEH / JEHOVAH) INCARNATED INTO HUMAN FLESH THROUGH MARY AT BETHLEHEM AND WAS CALLED - JESUS.

HE WAS NOT A TRINITY GOD.

Read: Genesis 1:1-31; 2:1-3; Exodus 3:13-14; 6:1-3; Isaiah 43:10-11; 49:16; John 5:39,46; 8:56-58; Revelation 21:67.

JESUS WAS THE YAHWEH (JEHOVAH) OF ABRAHAM, ISAAC, AND JACOB, <u>BEFORE</u> HIS INCARNATION INTO HUMAN FLESH THROUGH MARY AT BETHLEHEM.

- JESUS, HE WAS AND IS THE ONLY GOD.
- HE WAS THE GOD (YAHWEH / JEHOVAH) OF ABRAHAM, ISAAC, AND JACOB, WHO SPOKE TO MOSES AT THE BURNING BUSH. (Exodus 3:13-14; 6:1-3; John 5:39, 46; John 8:56-58).
- HE WROTE THE TEN COMMANDENTS ON TWO TABLETS OF STONE. (Exodus 20:1-17; 31:18).
- HE SITS ON THE THRONE IN HEAVEN.
- THAT MEANS, THERE IS <u>NO SUCH THING</u> AS A TRINITY GOD SITTING ON THE THRONE. Period!
- Read – Genesis 1:31-2:1-3; Exodus 3:13-14; 6:1-3; 20:1-3; Isaiah 43:10; 44:6, 24; 49:16; BEFORE Reading Revelation Chapters 4 and 5; Revelation 21:6-7.

Compiled by: Metusela F. Albert

Compiled by: Metusela F. Albert

THE JEWS BELIEVED IN <u>ONE GOD</u>. THEIR ONE GOD WAS THE GOD OF ABRAHAM, ISAAC, AND JACOB. THEIR ONE GOD DELIVERED THEM FROM SLAVERY IN EGYPT AND WROTE THE TEN COMMANDMENTS AND GAVE THROUGH MOSES ON MOUNT SINAI.

THEIR ONE GOD WAS THE GOD WHO CREATED HEAVEN AND EARTH IN SIX DAYS AND RESTED ON THE SEVENTH DAY. HE WAS <u>NOT</u> A TRINITY GOD. – Genesis 1:1-31; 2:1-3; Exodus 20:8-11.

JESUS WAS THE ELOHIM (YAHWEH / JEHOVAH) WHO WROTE THE TEN COMMANDMENTS.

THE ONLY EVERLASTING GOD.

1. The EVERLASTING <u>GOD</u> who created heaven and earth, created the light. HE was JESUS, the light of the world – Genesis 1:1-3; John 8:12.

2. The EVERLASTING CREATOR who made heaven and earth in six days and rested on the seventh day was JESUS, the LORD of the Sabbath – Genesis 1:1-31; 2:3, Exodus 20:8-11 – Mark 2:27, 28.

3. The EVERLASTING <u>CREATOR</u> of heaven and earth became the GOD of Abraham, and was called – "I AM THAT I AM." HE was JESUS - Exodus 3:13-14; John 5:39-46; 8:56-58.

4. The EVERLASTING GOD of Abraham was also called "JEHOVAH." HE was JESUS – Exodus 3:13-14; 6:1-3; John 5:39-46.

5. The EVERLASTING GOD of Abraham who delivered the children of Israel from slavery in Egypt wrote the Ten Commandments on Two Tablets of Stone at Mount Sinai. HE was JESUS – Exodus 20:1-17; 31:18; John 14:15.

6. Therefore, JESUS was <u>NOT</u> the Son of GOD in the Old Testament era.

7. There was <u>no such thing</u> as GOD had a Son called JESUS in heaven before the INCARNATION through Mary at Bethlehem.

8. And there was <u>no such thing</u> as a Trinity GOD or a Triune GOD, in heaven.

....

JESUS WAS THE GOD OF ABRAHAM— "I AM THAT I AM."

• Exodus 3:13-14

• ¹³ And Moses said unto God, "Behold, when I come unto the children of Israel and shall say unto them, 'The God of your fathers hath sent me unto you,' and they shall say to me, '<u>What is His name</u>?' what shall I say unto them?"

• ¹⁴ And God said unto Moses, "<u>I AM THAT I AM</u>." And He said, "Thus shalt thou say unto the children of Israel, '<u>I AM</u> hath sent me unto you.'"

• John 5:39 – JESUS said,

• "Search the Scriptures, for in them ye think ye have eternal life; and <u>it is they which testify of Me</u>.

COMPILED BY: METUSELA F. ALBERT.

THE FIRST COMMANDMENT

• Exodus 20:1-3 THIS IS NOT A TRINITY GOD NOR A DUALITY GOD.

• 1. And <u>God</u> spoke all these words, saying:

• ² "<u>I am the LORD thy God</u>, who have brought thee out of the land of Egypt, out of the house of bondage. READ THE SINGULAR PRONOUN

• ³ "<u>Thou shalt have no other gods before Me</u>

Compiled by: Metusela F. Albert

The GOD who wrote the Ten Commandments was the same GOD who spoke to Abraham, Moses, Isaiah, and the other Prophets.

HE WAS JESUS, THE ALPHA AND OMEGA.

EXPLANATION

The children of Israel knew only <u>one GOD</u>. He was the Almighty GOD of Abraham who created heaven and earth. He delivered them from slavery in Egypt. After delivering the Hebrew people from slavery in Egypt, they crossed the Red Sea and came to Mount Sinai. And He wrote the Ten Commandments on two tablets of Stone and gave through Moses.

CHAPTER 4

ELOHIM (YAHWEH /JEHOVAH) <u>INCARNATED</u> INTO HUMAN FLESH AND WAS CALLED – JESUS, THE SON OF GOD.

THE GOD OF ABRAHAM
(ELOHIM / YAHWEH / JEHOVAH)
INCARNATED
INTO HUMAN FLESH THROUGH MARY AT BETHLEHEM AND WAS CALLED - JESUS.

HE WAS NOT A TRINITY GOD.

Read: Genesis 1:1-31; 2:1-3; Exodus 3:13-14;6:1-3; Isaiah 43:10-11; 49:16; John 5:39,46; 8:56-58; Revelation 21:67.

Compiled by: Metusela F. Albert

THE GOD WHO SPOKE TO PROPHET ISAIAH IS THE ONLY ONE GOD IN HEAVEN. HE IS JESUS!

- Isaiah 43:10
- 10 Ye are my witnesses, saith the LORD, and my servant whom I have chosen: that ye may know and believe me, and understand that I am he: before me there was no God formed, neither shall there be after me.

THE REDEEMER OF ISRAEL

- Isaiah 44:6
- 6 Thus saith the LORD the King of Israel, and his redeemer the LORD of hosts; I am the first, and I am the last; and beside me there is no God.

THE REDEEMER / SAVIOR / SIN BEARER

THE CREATOR

- Isaiah 44:24
- 24 Thus saith the LORD, thy redeemer, and he that formed thee from the womb, I am the LORD that maketh all things; that stretcheth forth the heavens alone; that spreadeth abroad the earth by myself;

THE PROPHECY OF HIS DEATH AT CALVARY BY CRUCIFIXION.

- Isaiah 49:16

THIS IS NOT A TRINITY GOD NOR A TIUNE GOD

- 16 Behold, I have graven thee upon the palms of my hands; thy walls are continually before me.

THE CREATOR (ELOHIM) BECAME HUMAN FLESH THROUGH MARY BY INCARNATION.

JESUS WHO WAS YAHWEH, HUMBLY TOOK THE ROLE OF THE SON OF GOD WHEN HE BECAME HUMAN LIKE US.

AN AMAZING GRACE ACT.

CHAPTER 5

ELOHIM (YAHWEH / JEHOVAH) DID <u>NOT</u> HAVE A SON IN HEAVEN CALLED – JESUS.

NOTE: The Prophet may <u>repeat</u> what GOD said to the people. In that case, the Prophet is reiterating GOD'S word. . . . For example, when Moses repeated what God said in Exodus 20:1-3, to the people. That is <u>God's word</u> by the Prophet Moses to the people.

Compiled by: Metusela F. Albert

Therefore, what GOD said in Exodus 20:1-3 was GOD'S word.

//

NOTE: THE WORDS THAT PROCEEDED OUT OF GOD'S MOUTH ARE <u>GOD'S WORD</u>.

For example, in Genesis 1:3 - <u>GOD said</u>, "Let there be light."

That is GOD'S Word.

....

Those who read the BIBLE should try and understand <u>the difference</u> between "What GOD said to the Prophet," from "What the Prophet said to GOD," because <u>the Prophet's words are <u>not</u> GOD'S Word.</u>

....

REMEMBER THIS POINT. Satan's words as recorded in the BIBLE are <u>not</u> GOD'S Word. Therefore, the Bible is <u>not</u> GOD'S Word.

....

TAKE NOTE: If you never understood the simple explanation made above in regard to what refers to <u>GOD'S Word</u>, then definitely you are going to misunderstand the content and purpose of this Book.

....

I WILL REPEAT THE POINT:

What GOD said to the Prophets in the Old Testament about Himself, being the only One GOD, the Everlasting FATHER, did <u>NOT</u> contradict. Therefore, when you read the <u>Old Testament</u>, always ask yourself, "What did GOD say to the Prophets about who HE was?" – (Isaiah 7:14; 9:6).

In the <u>New Testament</u>, ask yourself, "What did JESUS say to the disciples about who HE was?" – (John 5:39, 46; 8:56-58).

....

DON'T JUDGE A BOOK BY ITS COVER.

This is a book that you <u>cannot</u> judge by its cover.

Thank you for having an open mind to read this Book and learn of the CONTRADICTIONS by John, Peter, James, Paul, etc.

Of course, many Professed Christians have <u>no clue</u> of the Contradictions in the New Testament.

DO YOU KNOW WHY?

It is because they have believed that everything written in the BIBLE are GOD'S Word. Therefore, unconsciously in an indirect way, they have believed that Satan's words in the Bible are GOD'S Word. That is a very simple contradiction of making the BIBLE become GOD'S Word.

They called <u>the BIBLE = "GOD'S WORD."</u> Indirectly, they have made Satan's Words as recorded in the BIBLE become GOD'S Word. They failed to understand that <u>GOD'S Word</u> are the words that He spoke to the Prophets.

They know very well that Satan's Words are <u>not</u> the Words of GOD, but their expression referring to the Bible as GOD'S Word made Satan's words in the BIBLE become GOD'S Word.

PLEASE LISTEN CAREFULLY.

The <u>Prophet's words</u> in his conversation with GOD, are <u>not</u> GOD'S Word. GOD and the Prophet are two distinct people.

....

I can assure you that you will <u>not</u> be the same person in your understanding of YAHWEH (ELOHIM / JEHOVAH) in the BIBLE, after reading this Book. Though you are going to learn of the Contradictions in the New Testament by John, Peter, James, and Paul, however, <u>your faith will be made much stronger because of what GOD said about Himself to the Prophets</u> – (Exodus 3:13-14; Isaiah 43:10-11).

....

After reading this Book carefully, believe me, your understanding of the Contradictions will make you a better person in <u>HOW</u> to read the Scriptures. Your faith will grow much stronger, and your desire to read the Old Testament will increase.

Of course, your faith and understanding of the GOD of the Old Testament which was JESUS, would make you a better student of the BIBLE. Your radar in detecting the contradiction by the writers in the New Testament will soar above the average Professed Christian.

....

LET'S BE VERY CLEAR.

GOD DID <u>NOT</u> CONTRADICT AT ALL.

I said, "The BIBLE Contradicts." I did <u>not</u> say, "GOD Contradicts."

THE CRUCIAL POINT:

It was John, Peter, James, and Paul, who contradicted the GOD of the Old Testament because they did <u>not</u> know that JESUS was the ELOHIM (YAHWEH / JEHOVAH) <u>of Abraham</u> in the Old Testament who came in human flesh <u>by INCARNATION</u> through Mary at Bethlehem – (04 B.C.).

They did <u>NOT</u> know that JESUS was the ELOHIM (YAHWEH / JEHOVAH) who <u>created</u> heaven and earth in six days, and rested on the seventh day. Prior to the INCARNATION through Mary at Bethlehem, JESUS was the <u>Almighty GOD</u> (ELOHIM / YAHWEH / JEHOVAH) of Abraham, Isaac, and Jacob.

JESUS was "the GREAT I AM THAT I AM" who spoke to Moses at the burning bush – (Exodus 3:13-14).

In other words, JESUS was <u>not</u> the Son of Abraham's GOD in the Old Testament. HE was <u>not</u> the Son of YAHWEH / JEHOVAH. . . . HE was JEHOVAH.

LET ME SAY IT ONE MORE TIME.

JESUS was the everlasting GOD (ELOHIM / YAHWEH / JEHOVAH) of Abraham, Isaac, and Jacob who created heaven and earth in six days and rested on the seventh day. The GOD (ELOHIM / YAHWEH / JEHOVAH) of Abraham did <u>not</u> have a begotten Son called JESUS, in heaven.

....

Dear Reader, stay tuned and start your journey through this Book that will clarify who JESUS was in the Old Testament. . . . HE <u>alone</u> is our only GOD in heaven, the GOD (ELOHIM / YAHWEH / JEHOVAH) of Abraham, Isaac, and Jacob. HE is <u>not</u> a Trinity GOD. And HE is <u>not</u> a Triune GOD.

....

FIRST THINGS FIRST.

The first five (5) Chapters of this Book will deal with the truth about JESUS, our only GOD (ELOHIM / YAHWEH / JEHOVAH), in heaven.

And the last ten (10) Chapters of this Book will show the contradictions by the New Testament writers who did <u>not</u> understand who JESUS was in the Old Testament, before His INCARNATION into human flesh through Mary at Bethlehem.

....

Take NOTE of this very important point:

When you fully come to a good understanding that JESUS was the Eternal GOD (Elohim / Yahweh / Jehovah) of Abraham, Isaac, Jacob, and the Prophets, who created heaven and earth in six days and rested on the seventh day, <u>only then</u> you would be able to notice the contradictions made by John, James, Peter, and Paul, in the New Testament.

....

I often tell others, "When you know the truth, you will easily know the error. But if you don't know the truth, then you won't know the error."

....

SO, WHAT IS THE TRUTH THAT YOU MUST KNOW FIRST, IN ORDER TO KNOW THE CONTRADICTION BY JOHN, PETER, JAMES, AND PAUL????

ANSWER: First, you need to understand that JESUS was the LORD GOD (ELOHIM / YAHWEH / JEHOVAH) who created heaven and earth in six days and rested on the seventh day. HE was the ELOHIM (YAHWEH / JEHOVAH) who humbly took human flesh through Mary at Bethlehem by INCARNATION, and died at Calvary to pay for the penalty of sin. ELOHIM (YAHWEH / JEHOVAH) became our Redeemer / Savior, in human flesh. In other words, JESUS was <u>not</u> the Son of GOD in heaven because HE was GOD (ELOHIM / YAHWEH/ JEHOVAH).

THE POINT IS REPEATED BELOW SO THAT YOU DON'T MISS IT.

1. GOD (ELOHIM / YAHWEH / JEHOVAH) gave <u>himself</u> to die at Calvary.

2. GOD (ELOHIM / YAHWEH / JEHOVAH) did <u>not</u> have a begotten Son in heaven.

3. GOD (ELOHIM / YAHWEH / JEHOVAH) did <u>not</u> give birth to a begotten Son in heaven.

4. GOD (ELOHIM / YAHWEH / JEHOVAH) gave <u>no Son called JESUS</u> to die at Calvary. (NO such thing as two beings existed in heaven).

5. GOD (ELOHIM / YAHWEH / JEHOVAH) gave <u>himself</u> to die at Calvary. (There was only <u>one</u> divine being).

6. GOD (ELOHIM / YAHWEH / JEHOVAH) <u>incarnated</u> into human flesh through Mary at Bethlehem, and was called <u>the Son of GOD</u> – (Luke 1:35).

//

IMPORTANT POINT:

In the Old Testament era, GOD (ELOHIM / YAHWEH / JEHOVAH) did <u>not</u> have a begotten Son called – JESUS. HE was the everlasting Father of the Children of Israel. HE was the "I AM" who spoke to Moses at the burning bush – (Exodus 3:13-14; John 8:56-58).

JESUS was the eternal <u>GOD the Father</u> (ELOHIM / YAHWEH / JEHOVAH), the GOD of Abraham, Isaac, and Jacob, who *<u>incarnated</u>* into human flesh through Mary at Bethlehem and was called – the Son of GOD – (Isaiah 9:6; Luke 1:35).

NOTE: IT WAS THE FATHER WHO BECAME THE SON OF GOD BY INCARNATION THROUGH MARY AT BETHLEHEM.

....

NOBODY HAS SEEN GOD IN THE OLD TESTAMENT TIME.

....

IN ORDER FOR GOD TO DIE AT CALVARY AS OUR SIN BEARER, HE HAD TO BE <u>INCARNATED</u> INTO HUMAN FLESH LIKE US, AND THE JEWS <u>SAW HIM</u> IN HUMAN FLESH ONLY.

UNFORTUNATELY, THEY REJECTED HIM AND KILLED HIM. . . . EVEN THOUGH HE HAD THE POWER TO DESTROY THEM, YET HE HUMBLY GAVE HIS LIFE, <u>AS PROPHESIED IN THE BOOK OF ISAIAH</u>. (Isaiah 7:14; 49:16; 53:1-10).

....

THE TRUTH MUST BE REITERATED IN SIMPLE LANGUAGE.

Once you fully grasp the truth that JESUS was the Everlasting GOD the FATHER (ELOHIM / YAHWEH / JEHOVAH) who created heaven and earth as in Genesis 1:1-31 and Genesis 2:1-3, only THEN you would easily notice the Contradictions by the other writers in the New Testament who advocated that JESUS was the SON of GOD from eternity <u>before</u> the angels existed.

Dear Professed Christians, don't be afraid to learn and accept <u>new truth if proven to be correct.</u> But reject Old and New teachings that are incorrect. Avoid being ignorant if truth is revealed and tested.

....

After reading this Book, all misunderstanding regarding GOD (ELOHIM / YAHWEH / JEHOVAH), the GOD of Abraham, should diminish.

I can assure you that you will <u>not</u> believe again in the TRINITY and TRIUNE GOD theories which misled many established denominations.

....

I would like to remind you again that GOD did <u>not</u> contradict himself in His conversations with the Prophets in the Old Testament.

....

SO, HOW DID THE CONTRADIICTION COME ABOUT???

It was John, Peter, James, and Paul, in the New Testament that contradicted what GOD said in the Old Testament about himself because they did <u>not</u> know that JESUS was the GOD of Abraham who humbly took human flesh through Mary at Bethlehem by INCARNATION.

Unfortunately, they believed that GOD the FATHER gave birth to a begotten Son called JESUS, in heaven. They failed to understand the INCARNATION of GOD through Mary at Bethlehem.

John, Peter, James, and Paul believed in <u>one</u> GOD, the GOD of Abraham. Amen! Good! Excellent!

BUT, they failed to understand the Prophecies of YAHWEH becoming the Son of GOD through a VIRGIN woman, to die at Calvary – (Isaiah 9:6; 7:14; 53:1-10).

They did <u>not</u> know that JESUS was the GOD of Abraham who came in human flesh through Mary at Bethlehem through the INCARNATION process to enable Him to die at Calvary, as our Sin Bearer / Redeemer / Savior.

We who live in 2023, should not repeat the same mistake they did. We are enlightened much better now because of the availability of the written Scriptures.

....

HERE IS THE THING. They did <u>not</u> understand the INCARNATION doctrine about our only GOD who took human flesh through Mary at Bethlehem and became our Sin-Bearer / Savior, at Calvary. They did <u>not</u> understand the <u>two natures</u> of JESUS while HE was in human flesh. While in human flesh at Bethlehem, HE was still divine. HE did <u>not</u> cease from being divine while in human flesh.

They did <u>not</u> understand the Prophecy in the Book of Isaiah regarding the coming of the Messiah, as a human being through a Virgin Woman – Isaiah 7:14; 9:6. Thus, they fulfilled the prophecy about their rejection and Crucifixion of the Messiah – Isaiah 49:16; 53:1-10.

They (John, Peter, Paul, etc.) <u>failed</u> to declare that the Everlasting GOD (ELOHIM / YAHWEH / JEHOVAH) of Abraham became human flesh through Mary at Bethlehem and was called JESUS.

When they spoke of GOD, they referred to the GOD (ELOHIM / YAHWEH / JEHOVAH) of Abraham <u>as a separate divine being</u> from JESUS. They referred to the GOD of Abraham <u>and his Son</u> (JESUS), as <u>TWO DISTINCT</u> persons. That is the "<u>DUALITY</u>" doctrine. (1 + 1 = 1). They referred to the Holy Spirit as <u>another distinct being</u>, a <u>third</u> being which endorses the TRINITY GOD theory =

(1 + 1 + 1 = 1 GOD). And most Professed Christians and Churches failed to understand who JESUS was in the Old Testament era.

THAT IS WHY THIS BOOK IS WRITTEN TO HIGHLIGHT THE CONTRADICTIONS IN THE BIBLE.

FURTHEMORE, THIS BOOK IS ALSO WRITTEN TO CLARIFY THE TRUTH ABOUT OUR EVERLASTING GOD WHO BECAME HUMAN FLESH.

....

The TRUTH is reiterated in FOURTEEN (14) different ways below so that the reader understands it better, and does not miss the point about JESUS.

1. GOD (HIMSELF) BECAME HUMAN FLESH BY INCARNATION THROUGH MARY AT BETHLEHEM (04 B.C.). ONLY ONE PERSON, NOT TWO PERSONS.

2. THERE IS NO SUCH THING AS, THE SON OF GOD BECAME HUMAN FLESH.

3. THERE IS NO SUCH THING AS, GOD THE SON BECAME HUMAN FLESH.

4. GOD DID NOT HAVE A SON IN HEAVEN BEFORE THE INCARNATION.

5. GOD DID NOT GIVE BIRTH TO A SON, IN HEAVEN.

6. GOD BEGAT NO BEGOTTEN SON, IN HEAVEN.

7. GOD CREATED NO BEGOTTEN SON, IN HEAVEN.

8. GOD THE FATHER AND JESUS ARE NOT TWO DISTINCT PERSONS.

9. NO PREGNANT GOD GAVE BIRTH TO A SON CALLED – JESUS, IN HEAVEN.

10. THE HOLY SPIRIT IS THE SPIRIT OF JESUS, NOT A THIRD PERSON.

11. THERE IS NO SUCH THING AS A DUALITY GOD.

12. THERE IS NO SUCH THING AS A TRINITY GOD.

13. THERE IS NO SUCH THING AS A TRIUNE GOD.

14. THERE IS NO SUCH THING AS GOD THE FATHER, GOD THE SON, AND GOD THE HOLY SPIRIT, MAKING UP ONE GOD.

//

The New Testament writers did <u>not intent</u> to contradict against what GOD said in the Old Testament. It was due to their lack of understanding about the GOD (YAHWEH / JEHOVAH) of Abraham at the time they wrote, and that makes the BIBLE to contradict itself.

It was their lack of knowledge of the GOD of Abraham who became human flesh. They did not know that JESUS was the GOD (ELOHIM / YAHWEH / JEHOVAH) of Abraham.

They failed to understand the prophecies in the Book of Isaiah about the <u>INCARNATION</u> of GOD into human flesh.

Today, most Protestant Churches have <u>not</u> understood it, and that is why they did <u>not</u> know of the Contradictions by John, Peter, James, Paul, etc.

Only when we come to a good understanding of the Everlasting GOD (ELOHIM / YAHWEH / JEHOVAH) of the Old Testament that HE was JESUS before his INCARNATION through Mary at Bethlehem, then we can easily recognize the CONTRADICTIONS made by the New Testament writers like John, Peter, James, and Paul.

In other words, we are to TEST the New Testament writers' belief about GOD, <u>by what GOD said</u> about himself to the Prophets in the Old Testament.

For example, read what GOD said to Moses about HIMSELF, ... Scriptures: Genesis 12:1-3; Exodus 3:13-14; 6:1-3; Isaiah 43:10-11; 44:6; 24; 49:16.

Let me say it again, in case you still did <u>not</u> get it. We are to TEST what the disciples and Paul wrote in the New Testament about GOD, by what GOD said to the Prophets in the Old Testament, <u>about Himself</u>.

YAHWEH was JESUS who came in human flesh. Read what JESUS said - (Luke 24:27).

"And beginning with Moses and all the prophets, <u>He expounded unto them in all the Scriptures the things concerning Himself."</u>

If you still did <u>not</u> understand it to this point, then you need to return and re-read again before you go any further from here. I can assure you, that by the time you finish reading this book, you will agree that THE BIBLE CONTRADICTS.

TAKE NOTE OF THIS VERY IMPORTANT POINT:

GOD DID <u>NOT</u> CONTRADICT WHAT HE SAID TO THE PROPHETS. . . . IT WAS THE NEW TESTAMENT WRITERS THAT CONTRADICTED WHAT GOD SAID ABOUT HIMSELF IN THE OLD TESTAMENT.

THE TRUTH IS:

JESUS WAS THE <u>ONLY EVERLASTING GOD</u> (ELOHIM / YAHWEH / JEHOVAH) WHO CREATED HEAVEN AND EARTH IN SIX DAYS AND RESTED ON THE SEVENTH DAY.

....

- **THE TRUTH IS:**
- **JESUS** was the <u>only</u> **GOD (ELOHIM / YAHWEH / JEHOVAH)** who created heaven and earth in six days and rested on the seventh day. . . . **HE became the GOD of Abraham who spoke to the Prophets in the Old Testament** . . .
- **HE later <u>INCARNATED</u> into human flesh through Mary at Bethlehem and became the Son of GOD. . . . YAHWEH had <u>NO</u> Son called JESUS in heaven before the angels existed.**
- **JESUS was NOT a Trinity GOD.**
- ....—
- **There was NO such thing as three living persons called – The Father, the Son (JESUS), and the Holy Spirit, existed in heaven before the angels existed.**

Compiled by: Metusela F. Albert

....

JESUS
IS OUR ONLY GOD IN HEAVEN.

Compiled by: Metusela F. Albert

- 1. JESUS WAS THE ELOHIM (YAHWEH / JEHOVAH) WHO CREATED HEAVEN AND EARTH, IN SIX DAYS.
- 2. JESUS WAS THE "I AM" WHO SPOKE TO MOSES AT THE BURNING BUSH.
- 3. JESUS WAS THE GOD OF ABRAHAM WHO WROTE THE TEN COMMANDMENTS, AT MOUNT SINAI.
- 4. THE HOLY SPIRIT WAS THE SPIRIT OF GOD WHICH WAS THE SPIRIT JESUS.
- 5. IT WAS ELOHIM (YAHWEH / JEHOVAH) WHO TOOK HUMAN FLESH AND BECAME THE SON OF GOD BY INCARNATION THROUGH MARY AT BETHLEHEM. HE WAS THEN CALLED – JESUS, THE SON OF GOD.

....

- TAKE NOTE:
- 1. There is no such thing as a Trinity GOD, OR a Triune GOD, in heaven.
- 2. There is no such thing as three divine persons existing in heaven.
- 3. There is only <u>one divine person</u> in heaven, and He is JESUS.
- 4. The Holy Spirit is <u>not</u> a third person in heaven.
- 5. There was no such thing as GOD gave birth to a Son in heaven and called his name JESUS.
- Genesis 1:1-31; 2:1-3; Exodus 3:13-14; 6:1-3; Isaiah 43:10-11; 44:6; 49:16; John 5:3946; 8:56-58; Revelation 21:6-7.

Compiled by: Metusela F. Albert

Compiled by: Metusela F. Albert

CHAPTER 6

JOHN'S CONTRADICTION IN JOHN 1:1-14 AND JOHN 3:16.

....

Let's read the Scriptures – John 1:1-3, 14.

v 1. In the beginning was the Word, and the Word was <u>with</u> God, and <u>the Word was God</u>.

v 2. The same was in the beginning <u>with</u> God.

v 3. All things were made by Him, and without Him was not anything made that was made.

....

v 14. And <u>the Word was made flesh, and dwelt among us</u> (and we beheld His glory, the glory as of the <u>only Begotten of the Father</u>), full of grace and truth.

....

EXPLANATION

John, a disciple of JESUS, introduced his gospel by telling us of the presence JESUS (the WORD) <u>*with*</u> GOD from the beginning. When John wrote about GOD, he was referring to the GOD of Abraham, Isaac and Jacob. Even though John believed in the GOD of Abraham <u>as the only one GOD</u>, yet John declared that <u>the WORD</u> (JESUS), the begotten of the Father, <u>was also GOD</u>. Therefore, John advocated the "<u>TWO GODS</u>" theory in John 1:1. (NOTE: This was a Contradiction).

John also declared that it was JESUS, <u>the Son of GOD</u>, who created heaven and earth – (John 1:1-3, 14). This contradicted Genesis 1:1.

According to John, the GOD of Abraham and the Son of Abraham's GOD (JESUS) were two distinct GODS. Then John added that the Holy Spirit is also another GOD, as in 1 John 5:7.

In fact, the <u>DUALITY</u> GOD theory and the <u>TRINITY</u> GOD theory, both came out of John's writings.

NOTE: John did <u>not</u> know that JESUS was the GOD of Abraham who became human flesh by INCARNATION through Mary at Bethlehem. Unfortunately, Professed Christians made the same mistake by believing in what John wrote.

Many *Mainline Churches* and *Denominations* failed to TEST what John wrote by Genesis 1:1.

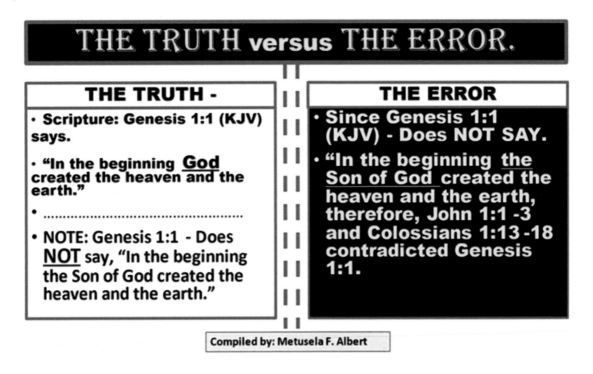

//

JOHN'S CONTRADICTION

Scripture: John 1:1-3, 14.

1. "In the beginning was <u>the Word</u>, and <u>the Word was with God</u>, and <u>the Word was God</u>.

[2] <u>The same</u> was in the beginning <u>with</u> God.

[3] <u>All things were made by Him</u>, and without Him was not anything made that was made."

....

[14] "And <u>the Word was made flesh</u>, and dwelt among us (and we beheld His glory, the glory as of <u>the only Begotten of the Father</u>), full of grace and truth."

....

EXPLANATION

According to John, JESUS was <u>the Word</u>, <u>the only begotten Son</u> of GOD who existed in heaven <u>*with*</u> the Father <u>*before*</u> anything was made. HE existed with the Father <u>*before*</u> the angels existed.

John declared that JESUS who was the Word <u>was also GOD</u>. When John spoke of the Father, he was referring to the GOD of Abraham. And John also referred to JESUS as the Son of Abraham's GOD.

John wrote that JESUS was <u>the Son of GOD (the Word)</u> who created heaven and earth.

John believed that JESUS who was <u>the Son of Abraham's GOD</u>, created all things.

NOTE: John did <u>not</u> understand that JESUS was the GOD of Abraham who became the Son of Abraham's GOD by <u>INCARNATION</u> through Mary at Bethlehem. There was only one person, <u>not</u> two persons.

THE TWO-GOD THEORY BY JOHN.

- John 1:1 - In the beginning was the Word, and the Word was <u>with</u> God, and the Word was God.

- NOTE: THE PREPOSITION WORD USED = "WITH."

- THAT MAKES THE MEANING TO BE "TWO-GODS".

COMPILED BY: METUSELA F. ALBERT.

According to John, the Son (JESUS) was the begotten of the Father from the beginning before the angels existed; therefore, the Son was born by the Father. GOD the Father existed *before* the Son. Since the Son of GOD was born by the Father, then the Son had a beginning. Hence, JESUS could <u>not</u> be Alpha and Omega.

John also declared that the Word <u>(the Son) was also GOD</u>. Therefore, GOD the Father and JESUS (the Son), were <u>TWO distinct GODS</u> from the beginning.

NOTE: The <u>*PREPOSITION*</u> used was – "WITH." That was a "<u>TWO-GODS</u>" theory introduced by the disciple John, in John 1:1-3. That is a CONTRADICTION.

It may not be intentional by John to advocate TWO-GODS, but his sincerity to declare JESUS to be a distinct being from the Father, and the use of the <u>PREPOSITION with,</u> made it a "TWO-GODS" theory.

And John later advocated the "TRINITY GOD" theory in 1 John 5:7 – (Three that bear record in heaven). That makes the Bible to contradict more.

....

LET'S LOOK AT THE <u>GREEK</u> TEXT SINCE THE NEW TESTAMENT WAS WRITTEN IN THE <u>GREEK</u> LANGUAGE. . . . TAKE NOTE OF <u>THE PREPOSITION</u> – "*WITH*" - AS USED IN JOHN 1:1.

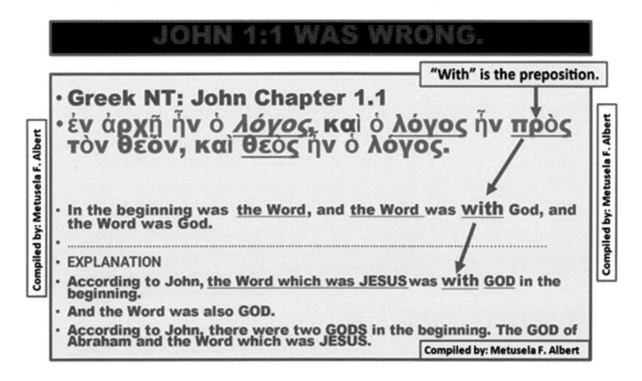

According to the disciple John, the GOD of Abraham and JESUS (THE WORD), were <u>TWO GODS</u> that existed from the beginning in heaven before the world was created.

John advocated that JESUS was the Son of Abraham's GOD who created heaven and earth.

THAT WAS A HUGE CONTRADICTION BY JOHN. AND CHRISTIANITY FAILED TO RECOGNIZE THE CONTRADICTIONS IN THE BIBLE. THAT IS THE REASON THIS BOOK IS WRITTEN TO EXLAIN THE CONTRADICTIONS.

HOWEVER, THE CONTRADICTIONS DID **NOT** MAKE GOD CONTRADICT **NOR** LESSEN OUR FAITH IN GOD WHO SPOKE TO THE PROPHETS.

WE CAN, AND SHOULD READ GOD'S WORD, AS RECORDED IN THE BIBLE.

NOW, OUR UNDERSTANDING OF THE CONTRADICTIONS AS HIGHLIGHTED IN THIS BOOK, MAKES US BECOME MORE CAREFUL TO LOOK FOR WHAT GOD SAID TO THE PROPHETS AND WHOSOEVER. AND WE ALSO DESIRE TO SEARCH FOR WHAT JESUS SAID TO WHOSOEVER, AS RECORDED IN THE NEW TESTAMENT.

Remember this, John did not know that JESUS was YAHWEH, the CREATOR, who became the GOD of Abraham, who later **incarnated** into human flesh through Mary at Bethlehem.

WHEN YOU KNOW THE TRUTH, YOU WILL EASILY KNOW THE ERROR.

THE TRUTH = THERE WAS ONLY ONE GOD. Isaiah 43:10-11.	JOHN ADVOCATED TWO GODS BECAUSE OF THE PREPOSITION – "WITH." John 1:1-3.
• Isaiah 43:10-11 • [10] "Ye are My witnesses," saith the LORD, "and My servant whom I have chosen, that ye may know and believe Me, and understand that I am He. Before Me there was no God formed, neither shall there be after Me. • [11] I, even I, am the LORD, and besides Me there is no savior."	• John 1:1-3 • 1. "In the beginning was the Word, and the Word was <u>with</u> God, and the Word was God. • [2] The same was in the beginning <u>with</u> God. • [3] All things were made by Him, and without Him was not anything made that was made." JOHN WAS WRONG Compiled by: Metusela F. Albert

CORRECTION TO JOHN 1:1

If John understood who JESUS was, then he would have written John 1:1, as – "In the beginning was the Word, and the Word was GOD, and the Word *incarnated* into human flesh through virgin Mary at Bethlehem, and was called JESUS, the Son of GOD."

CORRECTION TO JOHN 1:1.

JOHN 1:1 (KJV) WAS WRITTEN THIS WAY.	JOHN 1:1 SHOULD HAVE BEEN WRITTEN THIS WAY, IF HE UNDESTOOD ISAIAH 43:10-11; 44:6, 24.
• "In the beginning was the Word, and the Word was _with_ God, and the Word was God" • .... • NOTE: The PREPOSITION "with" which makes JESUS as another God besides the God of Abraham.	• "In the beginning was the Word, and the Word was GOD; and the Word _incarnated_ into human flesh through virgin Mary, and was called JESUS, the SON of GOD." • .... • NOTE: This theory refers to JESUS as the same person as the GOD of Abraham.

Compiled by: Metusela F. Albert

IF YOU ARE NOT CONVINCED YET OF JOHN'S CONTRADICTION, THEN READ WHAT JESUS SAID TO THE UNBELIEVING JEWS, IN JOHN 5:39, 5:46, and 8:56-58.

JESUS WAS THE GOD OF ABRAHAM CALLED "I AM" WHO SPOKE TO MOSES AT THE BURNING BUSH – (Exodus 3:13-14).

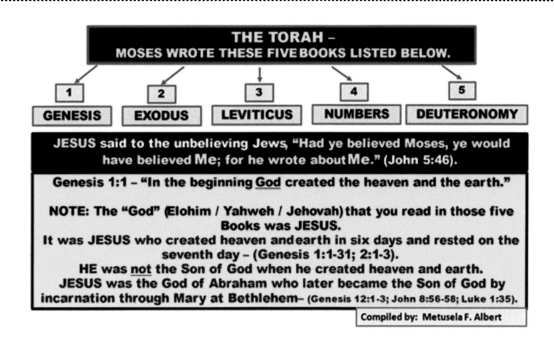

THE TORAH –
MOSES WROTE THESE FIVE BOOKS LISTED BELOW.

1	2	3	4	5
GENESIS	EXODUS	LEVITICUS	NUMBERS	DEUTERONOMY

JESUS said to the unbelieving Jews, "Had ye believed Moses, ye would have believed Me; for he wrote about Me." (John 5:46).

Genesis 1:1 – "In the beginning God created the heaven and the earth."

NOTE: The "God" (Elohim / Yahweh / Jehovah) that you read in those five Books was JESUS.
It was JESUS who created heaven and earth in six days and rested on the seventh day – (Genesis 1:1-31; 2:1-3).
HE was not the Son of God when he created heaven and earth.
JESUS was the God of Abraham who later became the Son of God by incarnation through Mary at Bethlehem– (Genesis 12:1-3; John 8:56-58; Luke 1:35).

Compiled by: Metusela F. Albert

JOHN'S CONTRADICTION IN JOHN 3:16

Scripture: For GOD so loved the world, that he gave his only begotten Son, that whosoever believeth in him should not perish, but have everlasting life.

....

If you believe in John 3:16 that GOD "BEGAT" a Son in heaven before the angels existed, then be prepared to answer three questions:

1. <u>WHO</u> WAS THE WIFE OF GOD THAT HE BEGAT THIS SON - JESUS?

2. IF GOD DID <u>NOT</u> HAVE A WIFE, THEN <u>HOW</u> DID GOD GET PREGNANT AND GAVE BIRTH TO A SON? . . .

3. DID GOD <u>GET PREGNANT</u> BY HIMSELF?

4. DID GOD <u>BEGAT</u> A SON? OR DID GOD <u>CREATE</u> A SON?

If you cannot give a satisfactory answer to those three questions, then listen to the truth and stop being ignorant from today.

WHAT IS THE TRUTH????

Most people don't know yet that YAHWEH / JEHOVAH, GOD the Father of Abraham, took human flesh through Mary at Bethlehem by <u>INCARNATION</u> and became the Son of GOD called - JESUS.

Prior to the <u>INCARNATION at Bethlehem</u>, GOD had <u>no</u> Son called JESUS, in heaven. GOD alone existed in heaven.

GOD DID <u>NOT</u> SEND A SON FROM HEAVEN BECAUSE GOD DID <u>NOT</u> HAVE A SON IN HEAVEN. IT WAS GOD HIMSELF THAT INCARNATED INTO HUMAN FLESH TO DIE AT CALVARY AS OUR SAVIOR / SIN BEARER.

Read - Exodus 3:13-14; 6:1-3; John 5:39, 46; 8:56-58; Revelation 1:17-18; 21:6-7. . . Further reading - Isaiah 43:10-11; 44:6, 24; 49:16.

NOTE: When the believers in JESUS come to a good understanding of the INCARNATION doctrine, then they will not believe in the Contradiction written by JOHN in John 1:1-3 and John 3:16, which advocated that GOD the Father BEGAT a Son; and both existed in heaven as <u>two distinct divine persons</u>.

In 1 John 5:7, John advocated <u>THREE DISTINCT PERSONS</u> existed in heaven. Who are they?

   1. The Father, 2. The Son, 3. The Holy Spirit = THREE that bear record in heaven.

John's contradiction about the Father, the Son, and the Holy Spirit are not recognized by the Protestant Churches of the 21st Century A.D. — WHY? Because most Christians already believed that everything you read in the Bible is <u>GOD'S word</u> and the BIBLE cannot contradict.

BEWARE:

THERE IS NO SUCH THING AS ABRAHAM'S GOD BEGAT A BEGOTTEN SON CALLED – "JESUS," IN HEAVEN - BEFORE THE ANGELS EXISTED.

THE BIBLE IS CONTRADICTORY = JOHN 3:16

- John 3:16 – "For God so loved the world, that He gave His only begotten Son, that whosoever believeth in Him should not perish, but have everlasting life." ....

1. According to John, God gave <u>birth</u> to a Son called JESUS, in heaven.
2. According to John, God and JESUS are <u>two distinct</u> divine beings.
3. According to John 1:1, JESUS was also God, = THE TWO GOD THEORY.
4. According to John, JESUS was <u>born TWICE</u>.
5. According to John, JESUS had a beginning, which made him not the Alpha and Omega.

NOTE: John did <u>not</u> know that JESUS was the GOD (YAHWEH / JEHOVAH) of Abraham who came in human flesh through Mary at Bethlehem by INCARNATION, died at Calvary as our Redeemer / Savior — Exodus 3:13 -14; 6:1 -3; Isaiah 7:14; 9:6; 43:10; John 5:39, 46; 8:56 -58, Matthew 1:21 -25; Luke 1:35, Revelation 21:6 -7..

Compiled by: Metusela F. Albert

TOO MUCH CONTRADICTION BY SO MANY CHURCHES AND PEOPLE.

1. Many Professed Christians believed that the FATHER and JESUS are TWO <u>distinct</u> divine beings that existed before the angels existed.

2. Many of them believed that the FATHER <u>begat</u> his Son before the angels existed.

3. They don't realize that they are telling us that the Son (JESUS) had a beginning since he was the begotten of the FATHER.

•TOO MUCH CONTRADICTION.

Compiled by: Metusela F. Albert

THERE IS NO SUCH THING AS ABRAHAM'S GOD <u>BEGAT</u> A SON CALLED – JESUS, IN HEAVEN – BEFORE THE ANGELS EXISTED.

....

THE TRUTH IS:

JESUS WAS THE ALMIGHTY GOD OF ABRAHAM, CALLED - "I AM THAT I AM," WHO INCARNATED INTO HUMAN FLESH THROUGH MARY AT BETHLEHEM – (Exodus 3:13-14; 6:1-3; Isaiah 43:10-11; 49:16; John 5:39-46; 8:56-58; Revelation 21:6-7).

....

WHEN YOU KNOW THE TRUTH, YOU WILL EASILY KNOW THE ERROR.

THE TRUTH = THERE WAS ONLY ONE GOD.

Isaiah 43:10-11.

- Isaiah 43:10-11
- [10] "Ye are My witnesses," saith the LORD, "and My servant whom I have chosen, that ye may know and believe Me, and understand that I am He. Before Me there was no God formed, neither shall there be after Me.
- [11] I, even I, am the LORD, and besides Me there is no savior."

JOHN ADVOCATED TWO GODS BECAUSE OF THE PREPOSITION – "WITH."

John 1:1-3.

- John 1:1-3
- 1. "In the beginning was the Word, and the Word was <u>with</u> God, and the Word was God.
- [2] The same was in the beginning <u>with</u> God.
- [3] All things were made by Him, and without Him was not anything made that was made." JOHN WAS WRONG

Compiled by: Metusela F. Albert

THE TRUTH ABOUT "JESUS."

- **JESUS** WAS THE <u>ONLY GOD</u> WHO CREATED HEAVEN AND EARTH. . .
- **HE** WAS **NOT** THE SON OF GOD IN HEAVEN WHEN HE CREATED HEAVEN AND EARTH IN SIX DAYS.
- BEFORE THE ANGELS EXISTED, GOD GAVE BIRTH TO NO SON IN HEAVEN CALLED – JESUS. . . .
- THEREFORE, JOHN 1:1-3 IS WRONG BECAUSE IT CONTRADICTED ISAIAH 43:10-11, AND 49:16.
- IT WAS "YAHWEH" (JEHOVAH) WHO TOOK HUMAN FLESH BY INCARNATION THROUGH MARY AT BETHLEHEM AND WAS CALLED – JESUS, THE SON OF GOD. (Luke 1:35).
- JESUS WAS THE YAHWEH OF ABRAHAM CALLED – "I AM THAT I AM" WHO SPOKE TO MOSES AT THE BURNING BUSH – Exodus 3:13-14; John 5:39, 46; 8:56-58.

Compiled by: Metusela F. Albert

Compiled by: Metusela F. Albert

Compiled by: Metusela F. Albert

Therefore, <u>be careful</u> when you read John 1:1-3, 14, John 3:16 and 1 John 5:7.

//

CHAPTER 7

JOHN'S CONTRADICTION IN 1 JOHN 4:1-19 AND 1 JOHN 5:7.

1 JOHN 4:1-19 . . . WHO IS ANTI-CHRIST?

1. When the disciple John wrote about GOD, he was referring to the GOD of Abraham as the only GOD in heaven.
2. And when John wrote about the Son of GOD, he was referring to the person called JESUS, who was born of Mary at Bethlehem.
3. Jesus often told the disciples that he was the Son of God who came down from heaven because the disciples did not believe in him as the MESSIAH.
4. John knew Joseph AND Mary were the Biological parents of JESUS.
5. However, John did not know of the INCARNATION whereby Joseph was not the Biological Father. (Mary was pregnant by GOD'S power).
6. John later believed in JESUS as the Messiah – John 4:22-27.
7. John did not know of the INCARNATION of YAHWEH into human flesh and that is why John further wrote that JESUS was the Son of God in 1 John 4:1-19. He wrote that anyone who does not believe in JESUS as the Son of God is Anti-Christ.
8. John failed to understand what JESUS said in John 5:39 – 46 and John 8:56-58.

Compiled by: Metusela F. Albert

THE CONTRADICTION BY JOHN IN 1 JOHN 5:7.

Scripture: "There are three that bear record in heaven, the Father, the Son, and the Holy Spirit."

....

EXPLANATION

This text, 1 John 5:7 - is contrary to what GOD said to the Prophet Isaiah about himself – (Isaiah 43:10 -11).

Read –

Isaiah 43:10-11 – There is only one God, none before Him and none after Him.

Isaiah 44:6, 24 – That God is Alpha and Omega.

Isaiah 9:6; 7:14 – That God is to be *incarnated* through a virgin Woman.

Isaiah 49:16; 53:1-10 – His death by *crucifixion* was predicted.

Exodus 20:1-17 – He wrote the Ten Commandments on two tablets of stone at Mt. Sinai.

Revelation 21:6-7 - HE spoke to John on the Island of PATMOS.

NOTE: The TRINITY GOD theory which is also called TRIUNE GOD was advocated by John in 1 John 5:7.

In fact, the source for the TRINITY GOD theory which says, "three in one," can be traced back to John's theology in 1 John 5:7.

In fact, the early Church failed to see the error that promotes three living persons in heaven, instead of one. And the PROTESTANT Churches of the 21ˢᵗ Century still have not seen the error.

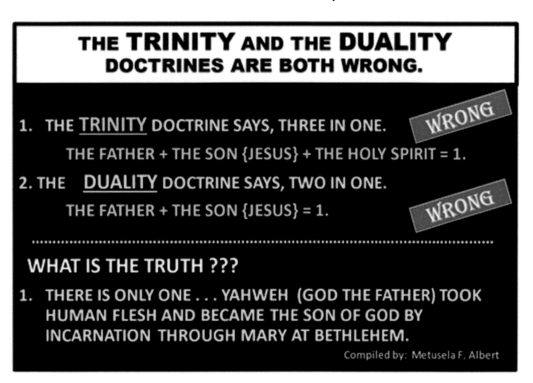

CHAPTER 8

PAUL'S CONTRADICTION IN ROMANS 8:34.

SCRIPTURE:

V34. "Who is he that condemneth? It is Christ that died, yea rather, that is risen again, who is even at the right hand of God, who also maketh intercession for us."

According to Paul, JESUS is sitting at GOD'S right-hand in heaven.

WHAT IS PAUL'S CONTRADICTION?

Paul did <u>not</u> know that JESUS was the GOD of Abraham. Of course, Paul did <u>not</u> know also that when JESUS was on earth in human flesh, he had <u>two natures</u> – the divine and the human nature.

JESUS' divine nature did not die because GOD cannot die, but his human nature died at Calvary. Therefore, when JESUS resurrected, he as GOD, resurrected himself – (John 2:19).

Remember? JESUS is the Resurrection and the Life – (John 11:25). HE resurrected Lazarus.

In heaven, JESUS was the Eternal GOD sitting on the THRONE.

CHAPTER 9

PAUL'S CONTRADICTION IN 1 CORINTHIANS 8:6.

1 Corinthians 8:6 (KJV).

⁶yet to us there is but <u>one God</u>, <u>the Father</u>, from whom are all things, and we in Him, and <u>one Lord Jesus Christ</u> by whom are all things, and we by Him.

....

EXPLANATION

Paul was correct in the notion of <u>one GOD</u>. But he was wrong in advocating JESUS as the One LORD, <u>a distinct divine Being from the GOD of Abraham.</u>

PAUL did not know that JESUS was the everlasting GOD of Abraham who took human flesh by the INCARNATION process through virgin Mary at Bethlehem.

....

THE GOD WHO SPOKE TO PROPHET ISAIAH IS THE ONLY ONE GOD IN HEAVEN. HE IS JESUS!

- Isaiah 43:10
- [10] Ye are my witnesses, saith the LORD, and my servant whom I have chosen: that ye may know and believe me, and understand that I am he: before me there was no God formed, neither shall there be after me.

- Isaiah 44:6
- [6] Thus saith the LORD the King of Israel, and his redeemer the LORD of hosts; I am the first, and I am the last; and beside me there is no God.

- Isaiah 44:24

- [24] Thus saith the LORD, thy redeemer, and he that formed thee from the womb, I am the LORD that maketh all things; that stretcheth forth the heavens alone; that spreadeth abroad the earth by myself;

- Isaiah 49:16

- [16] Behold, I have graven thee upon the palms of my hands; thy walls are continually before me.

THE CREATOR (ELOHIM) BECAME HUMAN FLESH THROUGH MARY BY INCARNATION.

JESUS WHO WAS YAHWEH, HUMBLY TOOK THE ROLE OF THE SON OF GOD WHEN HE BECAME HUMAN LIKE US.

AN AMAZING GRACE ACT.

CHAPTER 10

PAUL'S CONTRADICTION IN COLOSSIANS 1:15 -18.

¹⁵ He is the image of the invisible God, the firstborn of every creature.

¹⁶ For by Him were all things created that are in heaven and that are on earth, visible and invisible, whether they be thrones or dominions or principalities or powers: <u>all things were created by Him and for Him.</u>

¹⁷ And <u>He is before all things, and by Him all things consist.</u>

¹⁸ And He is the head of the body, the church. He is the beginning, the firstborn from the dead, that in all things He might have the preeminence.

....

EXPLANATION

THE TRUTH: Genesis 1:1 – "In the beginning GOD created the heavens and the earth."

It was <u>GOD</u> who created heaven and earth. It was <u>not</u> the Son of GOD who created heaven and earth. In fact, there was <u>no Son</u> of GOD when GOD created heaven and earth.

....

THE CONTRADICTION BY PAUL.

When Paul wrote his letter to the Church in Colossae, he never understood yet that JESUS was the <u>GOD</u> (ELOHIM / YAHWEH / JEHOVAH) who created heaven and earth.

Paul believed that JESUS was <u>the Son of GOD</u> who created heaven and earth. It was a subtle error by Paul.

When Paul wrote about GOD in his letters, he referred to the GOD of Abraham as the Father and Jesus was the Son of Abraham's GOD.

....

1. Paul believed that Jesus who was "<u>the Son of GOD</u>," created heaven and earth.

2. Paul believed that JESUS was <u>the Son of GOD</u> in heaven, with the FATHER <u>before</u> the angles existed.

3. Paul believed that JESUS was the begotten of the Father in heaven, <u>before</u> the angels existed.

4. Paul believed that when JESUS created heaven and earth, <u>he was the Son of GOD</u>, <u>not</u> the GOD of Abraham.

ACCORDING TO PAUL, THE SON OF GOD CREATED HEAVEN AND EARTH. . . . THAT CONTRADICTED GENESIS 1:1.

- COLOSSIANS 1:1317
- ¹³ <u>He</u> hath delivered us from the power of darkness, and hath translated us into the Kingdom of His dear Son,
- ¹⁴ in whom we have redemption through <u>His</u> blood, even the forgiveness of sins.
- ¹⁵ <u>He</u> is the image of the invisible God, <u>the firstborn of every creature.</u>
- ¹⁶ For by <u>Him were all things created that are in heaven and that are on earth, visible and invisible</u> whether they be thrones or dominions or principalities or powers: <u>all things were created by Him and for Him</u>
- ¹⁷ And <u>He is before all things, and by Him all things consist.</u>

Compiled by: METUSELA F. ALBERT

CHAPTER 11

PAUL'S CONTRADICTION IN 1 TIMOTHY 2:5.

⁵ For there is one God and one mediator between God and men, the man Christ Jesus, . . .

EXPLANATION

Paul who was a Pharisee, wrote from the perspective of the Sanctuary Building on earth and its services.

He was correct about the "ONE GOD," referring to the GOD of Abraham.

But He was wrong in advocating <u>a Sanctuary in heaven with two apartments</u> (the holy and the most holy). He was also wrong in promoting JESUS as the Mediator in heaven, a <u>distinct</u> divine being from GOD. In other words, Paul advocated that the GOD of Abraham was a distinct being from JESUS.

Unfortunately, Paul did <u>not</u> understand the following:

1. That JESUS was the <u>only GOD</u> in heaven.

2. That we pray directly <u>to JESUS who is our GOD, our heavenly FATHER.</u>

3. That there was <u>no</u> Sanctuary with <u>two</u> apartments (holy and most holy) in heaven.

4. That there was <u>no</u> Mediator <u>between GOD and man</u> in heaven, called JESUS.

NOTE: We as Professed Christians need to understand Paul's errors so that we don't fall into error.

When we know the truth about JESUS who was the GOD of Abraham and the Prophets, it is very easy to notice the error by Paul when he wrote that JESUS was the Son of GOD in heaven with the Father before the INCARNATION by Mary at Bethlehem.

Read Paul's Introduction of his 14 letters to the Churches and know where he stands in his belief about the Father and JESUS. Very Simple to recognize the errors.

THE GOD WHO SPOKE TO PROPHET ISAIAH IS THE ONLY ONE GOD IN HEAVEN. HE IS JESUS!

- Isaiah 43:10
- 10 Ye are my witnesses, saith the LORD, and my servant whom I have chosen: that ye may know and believe me, and understand that I am he: before me there was no God formed, neither shall there be after me.

- Isaiah 44:6
- 6 Thus saith the LORD the King of Israel, and his redeemer the LORD of hosts; I am the first, and I am the last; and beside me there is no God.
- Isaiah 44:24

- 24 Thus saith the LORD, thy redeemer, and he that formed thee from the womb, I am the LORD that maketh all things, that stretcheth forth the heavens alone; that spreadeth abroad the earth by myself;

- Isaiah 49:16

- 16 Behold, I have graven thee upon the palms of my hands; thy walls are continually before me.

THE CREATOR (ELOHIM) BECAME HUMAN FLESH THROUGH MARY BY INCARNATION.

JESUS WHO WAS YAHWEH, HUMBLY TOOK THE ROLE OF THE SON OF GOD WHEN HE BECAME HUMAN LIKE US.

AN AMAZING GRACE ACT.

CHAPTER 12

PAUL'S CONTRADICTION IN HEBREWS 1:1-2

1. Therefore, seeing we also are compassed about by so great a cloud of witnesses, let us lay aside every weight, and the sin which doth so easily beset us, and let us run with patience the race that is set before us,

^{2} looking unto Jesus, the author and finisher of our faith, who for the joy that was set before <u>Him</u> endured the cross, despising the shame, and <u>is sat down at the right hand of the throne of God.</u>

///

EXPLANATION

According To Paul, when JESUS ascended back to heaven after the resurrection, <u>HE sat on the right-hand of GOD.</u>

Paul repeated that theory in Romans 8:34. Read Chapter 8 of this Book.

When Paul talked of GOD, he was referring to the GOD of Abraham. Therefore, Paul did <u>not</u> know that the GOD of Abraham was JESUS. Therefore, there is no such thing as the Son of GOD was siting on the right hand of GOD in heaven.

....

In the above Scripture, Paul advocated the following <u>FALSE</u> beliefs:

1. That JESUS and the GOD of Abraham were <u>two distinct</u> beings.

2. That the GOD of Abraham was the only one sitting on the throne.

3. That JESUS was the Son of GOD in heaven, sitting on the right hand of the GOD of Abraham.

4. That JESUS was the Son of Abraham's GOD who came in human flesh and died at Calvary.

5. That JESUS was <u>born</u> (begat) in heaven by GOD the Father before the angels existed.

6. That GOD the Father, the GOD of Abraham, was self-existent, but <u>not</u> JESUS since he was GOD'S begotten Son in heaven before the angels existed.

7. That JESUS was the first-born of all creatures.

8. That JESUS was the image of the Invisible GOD.

9. That JESUS was the MEDIATOR in heaven between GOD and man.

10. That there was a Sanctuary in heaven with two apartments, the holy and most holy.

....

- **When PAUL talked about GOD the FATHER in his letters to the Churches, he referred to the GOD of Abraham, Isaac, and Jacob, as a <u>distinct being</u> from JESUS and the HOLY SPIRIT.**
- **Unfortunately, PAUL did NOT know that JESUS was the GOD of Abraham, Isaac, and Jacob.**
- **PAUL did NOT know that the HOLY SPIRIT was the SPIRIT of GOD which was the SPIRIT of JESUS.**
- **Therefore, becareful when you read PAUL'S writings about GOD the FATHER, JESUS, and the HOLY SPIRIT.**
- **Paul believed in THREE distinct persons in heaven, instead of ONE person.**

CHAPTER 13

PETER'S CONTRADICTION IN 1 PETER 1:3.

"Blessed *be* <u>the God and Father</u> of our Lord Jesus Christ, which according to his abundant mercy has begotten us again unto a lively hope unto the resurrection of Jesus Christ from the dead."

....

EXPLANATION

At the time of writing, Peter did <u>not</u> know yet that JESUS was the GOD of Abraham who came in human flesh by <u>incarnation</u> through Mary at Bethlehem.

Peter expressed that the GOD of Abraham was the Father of JESUS. Therefore, according to Peter, JESUS and the GOD of Abraham were <u>TWO DISTINCT DIVINE BEINGS</u>. Not only Peter, but the other disciples and Paul believed the same thing.

And most Churches and Professed Christians believed the same thing when it comes to the GOD of Abraham and JESUS.

THINK! THINK! THINK!

Many Professed Christians believed that the BIBLE cannot be wrong because they believed that everything written in the Bible is GOD'S Word.

Unfortunately, they failed to reason that Satan's words are recorded in the BIBLE. Therefore, making THE BIBLE GOD'S WORD, they are making Satan's words to be GOD'S WORD.

DON'T FORGET – The BIBLE is a Book that *contains* GOD'S spoken words to the Prophets, and the words of the Prophets, and others – Adam, Cain, Abel, Noah, Jethro, Moses, Aaron, Miriam, Joshua, Caleb, Rahab, Jezebel, Jesse, David, Solomon, Joab, Nebuchadnezzar, Elijah, etc.

In the New Testament, the BIBLE contains the words of JESUS, the words of Zechariah, Elizabeth, John the Baptist, Joseph and Mary, Nicodemus, Thomas, Phillip, Judas, Pilate, Mary, Martha, Lazarus, Matthew, Mark, Luke, John, Paul, James, Timothy, etc. We must be able to differentiate <u>what GOD said</u> from the words of others.

CHAPTER 14

JOHN'S CONTRADICTION IN REVELATION 1:8-11.

Revelation 1:1-8 (King James Version)

1 The Revelation of <u>Jesus Christ, which God gave unto Him</u> to show unto His servants things which must shortly come to pass. And He sent and signified it by His angel unto His servant John,

² who bore record of the Word of God, and of the testimony of Jesus Christ, and of all things that he saw.

³ Blessed is he that readeth, and they that hear the words of this prophecy, and keep those things which are written therein; for the time is at hand.

⁴ John, To the seven churches in Asia: Grace be unto you and peace from Him who is, and who was, and who is to come, and from the seven spirits which are before His throne;

⁵ and from Jesus Christ, who is the faithful witness, and the first-begotten of the dead, and the prince over the kings of the earth. Unto Him that loved us, and washed us from our sins in His own blood,

⁶ and <u>hath made us kings and priests unto</u> God and His Father, to Him be glory and dominion for ever and ever. Amen.

⁷ Behold, He cometh with clouds, and every eye shall see Him, and they also who pierced Him; and all kindreds of the earth shall wail because of Him. Even so. Amen.

8 "I Am Alpha And Omega, The Beginning And The Ending," saith the Lord, who is, and who was, and who is to come, the Almighty.

....

EXPLANATION

If you read carefully just the *first* verse of Revelation, you would have noticed that John introduced the reader to the Book of Revelation with the understanding that GOD the Father and JESUS were two distinct beings.

John who wrote the gospel of John, explicitly believed that the GOD of Abraham was a different person from JESUS – (John 1:1 and John 3:16 and 1 John 5:7).

And we noticed that John's belief about JESUS as GOD'S Son is seen again in his introduction of the Book of Revelation.

That notion about the FATHER and JESUS as two DISTINCT beings contradicted what JESUS said to John in Revelation 1:8, "I AM ALPHA and OMEGA, the BEGINNING and the ENDING." . . . JESUS was reminding John that HE was the ALPHA and OMEGA who spoke to Prophet Isaiah – (Isaiah 43:10-11; 44:6, 24).

JESUS reiterated again that He is the ALPHA AND OMEGA, in Revelation 1:17-18, 21:6-7.

....

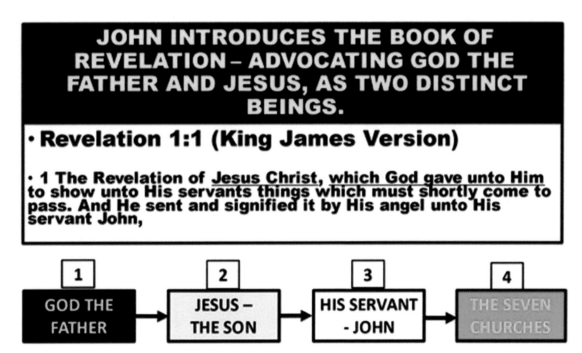

JESUS WAS THE ALPHA AND OMEGA THAT SAT ON THE THRONE.

- **Revelation 21:5-7**

- 5. And **He** that sat upon the throne said, *"Behold **I** make all things new."* And he said unto me, *" Write for these words are true and faithful."*

- 6. And **He** said unto me, *"It is done. I am Alpha and Omega, the beginning and the end. I will give unto him that is athirst of the fountain of the water of life freely.*

- *He that overcometh shall inherit all things; and **I** will be his God, and he shall be my son."*

- Isaiah 43:10-11; 44:6, 24; 49:16.

- NOTE: JESUS WAS NOT A TRINITY GOD.

Compiled by: Metusela F. Albert

(Compiled by: Metusela F. Albert)

Many professed Christians still have **not** understood yet that JESUS had to come in human flesh like us to die at Calvary as our Sin Bearer and Savior. IF JESUS did not take human flesh by INCARNATION, we would have no Sin Bearer / Savior. And we would all be lost.

Since JESUS was an eternal GOD, He cannot die. Nobody can kill Him. Period!

JESUS IS THE ONLY GOD IN HEAVEN. THERE IS NONE ELSE BESIDES HIM.

HE chose to take human flesh by the INCARNATION process through Mary at Bethlehem, to enable Him to die and save us.

Throughout His life of thirty-three and a half years, from the age of accountability, He was tempted in all points as we are, yet did not sin. . . . Halleluiah. Praise the LORD.

HAVE YOU HEARD THIS YET?

I heard someone said, "Had JESUS fallen into sin, He would need a Savior."

Really? Who would be the Savior for him? There is no one else besides Him in heaven, to save Him and us. HE alone is GOD.

1. THEN WHAT OTHER OPTION LEFT FOR JESUS AND MANKIND, IF HE SINNED?

An option is for JESUS to save us <u>in sin</u>. OR Abolish the Ten Commandments.

2. WHAT ELSE?

Then remove <u>the first death</u> that we inherited from Adam. No more death to anyone.

3. WHAT ELSE?

Then re-instate Lucifer and the fallen angels back to heaven.

....

TAKE NOTE OF THIS VERY IMPORTANT POINT:

JESUS was GOD, and HE had divine nature. . . . In the PLAN OF SALVAATION, JESUS took <u>human nature</u> like us and inherited <u>the first death</u> from his mother, Mary.

HE did <u>not</u> cease from being divine, but voluntarily took human nature upon his divine nature. While in human flesh, JESUS had <u>two natures</u>, the divine and the human. In human flesh like us, he was tempted in all points as we are, yet sinned not – (Hebrews 4:15).

He died at Calvary and resurrected after three days. But <u>his divine nature</u> cannot die, and did <u>not</u> die.

It was JESUS, the CREATOR of heaven and earth, who resurrected His own human body from the grave. HE is the Resurrection and the Life – John 2:19; 11:

CHAPTER 15

THE CONTRADICTION BY JAMES.

Scripture: James 1:1 – "James, a servant of God and of the Lord Jesus Christ, to the twelve tribes which are scattered abroad, greeting."

EXPLANATION

According to James, GOD was _a distinct person_ from JESUS. Therefore, the GOD of Abraham and JESUS were _two separate_ persons.

Unfortunately, James did <u>not</u> know that JESUS was the Almighty GOD of Abraham who incarnated into human flesh through Mary at Bethlehem.

James was sincere but wrong in his belief regarding GOD and JESUS. He failed to understand the INCARNATION doctrine.

NOTE: Professed Christians who believed that everything written in the Bible are GOD'S word, cannot see the contradiction.

When you read the OLD TESTAMENT and understand that the GOD of Abraham became human flesh, only then it helps you to notice the contradiction by the writers of the New Testament in regard to their understanding of GOD and JESUS, as <u>two distinct persons</u>, instead of one – the same person.

CHAPTER 16

WHO RESURRECTED JESUS? NOTE PAUL'S CONTRADICTION.

....

HEBREWS 12:1-2

1. Therefore, seeing we also are compassed about by so great a cloud of witnesses, let us lay aside every weight, and the sin which doth so easily beset us, and let us run with patience the race that is set before us,

² looking unto Jesus, the author and finisher of our faith, who for the joy that was set before Him endured the cross, despising the shame, and <u>is set down at the right hand of the throne of God.</u>

//

EXPLANATION

According To Paul, when JESUS ascended back to heaven after the resurrection, He went and sat on the right hand of GOD. . . . That means, JESUS was a distinct (separate) person from GOD. In other words, JESUS was <u>not</u> the GOD of Abraham, but the Son of Abraham's GOD.

When Paul spoke of GOD, he was referring to the GOD of Abraham. Therefore, that is the evidence that Paul did <u>not</u> know that the GOD of Abraham was JESUS.

Paul advocated the following beliefs about GOD the FATHER and JESUS.

    1.   That JESUS and the GOD of Abraham were <u>two distinct</u> beings.

2. That the GOD of Abraham was the one sitting on the throne, but not JESUS.

3. That JESUS was the Son of GOD in heaven, sitting <u>on the right hand</u> of the GOD of Abraham.

4. That JESUS was <u>born</u> in heaven by GOD the Father before the angels existed.

5. That JESUS was the Son of Abraham's GOD in heaven before the angels existed.

6. That JESUS was the Son of Abraham's GOD in heaven <u>who came down</u> and <u>incarnated</u> into human flesh through Mary at Bethlehem, and died at Calvary as the Savior.

7. That GOD the Father, the GOD of Abraham was self-existent, but <u>not</u> JESUS who was born by the Father before the angels existed.

8. That when JESUS ascended to heaven, He sat at the right-hand of GOD and became the Mediator between GOD and man.

9. That we pray to the Father (the GOD of Abraham) through the Son (JESUS) who is the Mediator between GOD and man.

10. That the Son of GOD created all things.

NOTE: THOSE 10 BELIEFS OF PAUL ARE ALL WRONG.

WHO IS THE HOLY SPIRIT?

1. The Holy Spirit is the Spirit of GOD – Genesis 1:2.

2. The Holy Spirit is <u>NOT</u> a third person NOR a third GOD.

3. Since JESUS is the only GOD in heaven, therefore, the Holy Spirit is the Spirit of JESUS.

4. JESUS is the person. The Holy Spirit is <u>NOT</u> the person.

5. Only when you have JESUS, then you have the Holy Spirit.

6. IF you don't have JESUS who is the person, then you can't have the Holy Spirit.

7. The Father, the Son, and the Holy Ghost are <u>NOT</u> three separate beings.

8. THERE WAS NO SUCH THING AS THREE PERSONS MAKING UP ONE GOD, IN HEAVEN.

....

Matthew 28:19-20 (KJV).

JESUS said to the disciples, "Go ye therefore, and teach all nations, baptizing them in the name of the Father, and of the Son, and of the Holy Ghost.

Teaching them to observe all things whatsoever I have commanded you: and, lo, I am with you always, even unto the end of the world. Amen."

DON'T MISS THIS: JESUS WAS THE FATHER IN THE OLD TESTAMENT. HE BECAME HUMAN FLESH THROUGH MARY AT BETHLEHEM BY THE <u>INCARNATION</u> PROCESS. HE WAS THE FATHER WHO BECAME THE SON BY INCARNATION. AND THE HOLY SPIRIT WAS THE SPIRIT OF JESUS. THERE

WAS ONLY ONE BEING, NOT TWO BEINGS. AND THERE WAS <u>NO THREE PERSONS</u> IN HEAVEN MAKING ONE GOD.

....

JESUS WAS **NOT** A TRINITY GOD. . . . CHECK OUT THE SINGULAR PRONOUN USED.

- Matthew 28:19-20 (KJV).
- JESUS said to the disciples, "Go ye therefore, and teach all nations, baptizing them in the name of <u>the Father</u>, and of <u>the Son</u>, and of <u>the Holy Ghost</u>.
- Teaching them to observe all things whatsoever <u>I</u> have commanded you: and, lo, <u>I</u> am with you always, even unto the end of the world. Amen."
- ....
- NOTE: JESUS WAS THE FATHER WHO INCARNATED INTO HUMAN FLESH THROUGH MARY AND BECAME THE SON OF GOD. . . . AND THE HOLY SPIRIT WAS THE SPIRIT OF JESUS.

Compiled by: Metusela F. Albert

HOW WOULD WE KNOW THAT THE APOSTLE JOHN CONTRADICTED???

First, find out <u>WHAT GOD said</u> about himself in the Old Testament to Prophet Isaiah?????

Then test what John said about GOD and JESUS.

Look at the diagram below.

THE TRUTH –

THE GOD OF ABRAHAM WAS THE ONLY GOD WHO LATER <u>INCARNATED</u> INTO HUMAN FLESH THROUGH MARY AT BETHLEHEM - CALLED JESUS CHRIST. . . YAHWEH GAVE HIMSELF TO DIE AT CALVARY. . . HE DID NOT HAVE A SON IN HEAVEN.

• Isaiah 43:10-11.
• Isaiah 44:6, 24.
• Isaiah 49:16.

THE CONTRADICTION BY JOHN

- John advocated the "Two Gods Theory." Read the preposition "<u>with</u>" used by John in John 1:1.

• John 1:1
• In the beginning was the Word, and the Word was <u>with</u> GOD, and the Word was GOD.

Compiled by: Metusela F. Albert

55

HOW DO WE KNOW THAT PETER WAS WRONG IN HIS BELIEF ABOUT JESUS AND GOD?

Compiled by: Metusela F. Albert – 08/27/2022

- When we come to a good understanding that JESUS was the GOD (YAHWEH / JEHOVAH) of Abraham and the prophets in the OLD TESTAMENT, hence, that gives us the understanding that Paul and the disciples were wrong in advocating JESUS as the Son of GOD in heaven before the angels existed.

- There is no such thing as God the Father gave birth to a begotten Son in heaven called – JESUS.

- THEREFORE, THERE IS NO SUCH THING AS A TRINITY GOD IN HEAVEN BECAUSE JESUS CHRIST WAS NOT, AND IS NOT A TRINITY GOD. . . .

- JESUS WAS NOT A TRIUNE GOD. HE WAS THE ALPHA AND OMEGA, HAD NO BEGINNING AND NO END.

- IT IS THAT SIMPLE.

Compiled by: Metusela F. Albert – 08/27/2022

GOD'S MATTHEMATICS versus SATAN'S.

- 1 + 1 + 1 = 3, NOT 1.
- 1 GOD + 1 GOD + 1 GOD = 3 GODS, NOT 1 GOD.
- 1 APPLE + 1 APPLE + 1 APPLE = 3 APPLES, NOT 1 APPLE.
- 1 PERSON + 1 PERSON + 1 PERSON = 3 PERSONS, NOT 1 GOD.
- GOD THE FATHER + GOD THE SON + GOD THE HOLY SPIRIT = 3 GODS.
- ....
- **NOTE: THE TRINITY GOD THEORY IS SATANIC.**
- ....
- **1 + 1 + 1 = 1, is a Satanic, man-made equation.**

Compiled by: Metusela F. Albert.

I hope this Book is of help to you as a reader, in your understanding of <u>what GOD said about Himself</u>, and what the New Testament authors said about GOD THE FATHER, JESUS, AND THE HOLY SPIRIT.

WHO IS THE HOLY SPIRIT?

Since JESUS was the only GOD of the children of Israel, then who was the Holy Spirit?

Was the Holy Spirit <u>a third person</u> in heaven? No!

The Holy Spirit was <u>the Spirit of GOD</u> – (Genesis 1:2). Since JESUS was the only GOD in heaven, therefore, the HOLY SPIRIT was <u>the SPIRIT of JESUS</u>.

NOTE: The HOLY SPIRIT was <u>not</u> a person <u>NEITHER</u> a third person or a third GOD in heaven.

JESUS was the COMFORTER who came in human flesh. It was the SPIRIT of JESUS that was present on earth after HE ascended to heaven. Nobody was able to see the Holy Spirit.

THE SPIRIT OF JESUS WAS <u>NOT</u> A THIRD PERSON.

....

IS THE HOLY SPIRIT A PERSON? NO!

1. The Holy Spirit is <u>NOT</u> a person.
2. The Holy Spirit is <u>NOT</u> a third person in heaven.
3. There is only <u>one person</u> that exists in heaven before the angels existed, and HE is GOD (JESUS).
4. JESUS IS THE PERSON. THE HOLY SPIRIT IS <u>NOT</u> THE PERSON.
5. THE HOLY SPIRIT IS THE SPIRIT OF GOD WHICH IS THE SPIRIT OF JESUS – (Genesis 1:2).
6. There is no such thing as three persons called– The Father, the Son, the Holy Spirit, existed in heaven before the angels existed.

Compiled by: Metusela F. Albert

THEREFORE, BEWARE OF THE CONTRADICTION BY THE DISCIPLE JOHN, IN 1 John 5:7, WHICH PROMOTES THREE DIVINE BEINGS EXISTING IN HEAVEN.

John did <u>not</u> intend to lie. He was sincere, yet wrong.

THERE IS <u>NO</u> SUCH THING AS THREE PERSONS BARE RECORD IN HEAVEN.

OF COURSE, THERE IS <u>NO</u> SUCH THING AS <u>A TRINITY GOD OR A TRIUNE GOD, SITTING ON THE THRONE IN HEAVEN.</u>

....

PAUL'S UNDERSTANDING OF GOD THE FATHER AND JESUS WAS WRONG.

WHY? HOW? IT IS BECAUSE THERE IS NO TWO PERSONS OR THREE PERSONS IN HEAVEN.

REMEMBER THIS: JESUS IS THE <u>ONLY GOD</u> IN HEAVEN, THEREFORE, THERE IS NO WAY THAT HE WAS SITTING ON THE RIGHT-HAND OF GOD IN HEAVEN.

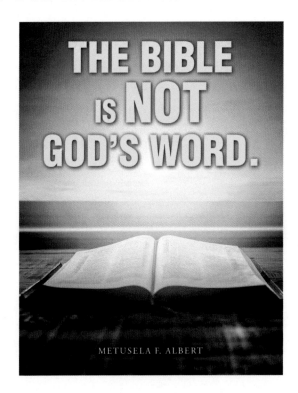

//

FURTHER READING OF THESE BOOKS WILL SURELY HELP ONE TO UNDERSTAND THE CONTRADICTIONS MUCH BETTER.

PUBLISHED ON MARCH 04, 2011

PUBLISHED ON JUNE 01, 2011

THERE IS NO TRINITY GOD IN HEAVEN.

BOOK - PUBLISHED ON DECEMBER 16, 2020

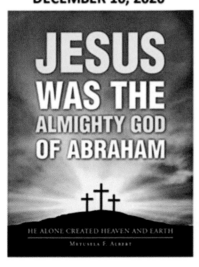

BOOK - PUBLISHED ON JANUARY 22, 2021

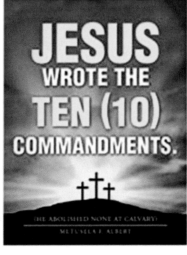

BOOK - PUBLISHED ON SEPTEMBER 12, 2021

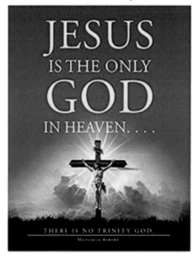

///

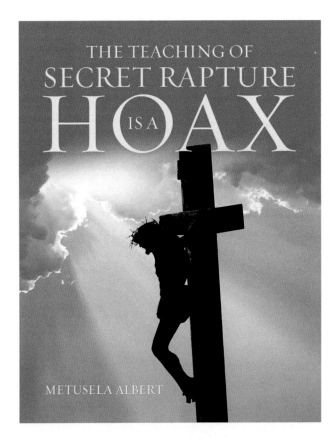

///

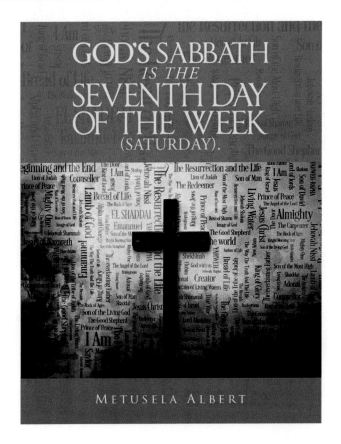

CONCLUSION

When you read the BIBLE, try and read the immediate and wider <u>context,</u> and take note of <u>the Singular Pronouns</u> used in the Old Testament in reference to GOD; and you would have a better understanding that the everlasting GOD who created heaven and earth in six days, was <u>not</u> a Trinity GOD.

Genesis 1:27 / Genesis 1:28 / Genesis 1:29 / Genesis 2:1-3 / Genesis 12:1-3 / Exodus 20:1-3.

When you have a good understanding that the everlasting GOD (ELOHIM / YAHWEH / JEHOVAH) who spoke to the Prophets in the Old Testament <u>was JESUS</u>, only then you would easily notice the CONTRADICTION of the BIBLE by the writings of John, Peter, James, and Paul, in regard to JESUS as the Son of GOD in heaven before the angels existed. They failed to understand the INCARNATION doctrine through virgin Mary at Bethlehem.

Any Scripture in the New Testament that advocates the notion that JESUS was the Son of GOD, the begotten of the Father, before the angels existed in heaven, <u>is a contradiction to what GOD said</u> in the Old Testament about Himself.

///

Genesis 2:1-3 = THE LORD OF THE SABBATH WAS NOT A TRINITY GOD. . . Read the Pronouns – "HE" and "HIS." . . . JESUS WAS NOT A TRINITY GOD.

- 1. Thus the heavens and the earth were finished, and all the host of them.

- 2 And on the seventh day **God** ended **His** work which **He** had made; and **He** rested on the seventh day from all **His** work which **He** had made.

- 3 And **God** blessed the seventh day and sanctified it, because in it **He** had rested from all **His** work which **God** created and made.

Compiled by: Metusela F. Albert

THANK YOU FOR CHOOSING TO READ THIS BOOK WITH AN OPEN MIND.

MAY GOD BLESS YOU ABUNDANTLY AND GIVE YOU GOOD HEALTH AND WEALTH TO FURTHER THE GOSPEL ABOUT JESUS CHRIST, OUR ONLY GOD IN HEAVEN, WHO CREATED US ALL.

HANISIOF. MOCE.

THE END

Printed in the United States
by Baker & Taylor Publisher Services